The Aging Population

Other Books of Related Interest:

Opposing Viewpoints Series

Medical Technology

Medical Testing

At Issue Series

Extending the Human Lifespan

Right to Die

Current Controversies Series

Social Security

"Congress shall make
no law . . . abridging
the freedom of speech,
or of the press."

First Amendment to the US Constitution

The basic foundation of our democracy is the First Amendment guarantee of freedom of expression. The Opposing Viewpoints Series is dedicated to the concept of this basic freedom and the idea that it is more important to practice it than to enshrine it.

I The Aging Population

Margaret Haerens, Book Editor

GREENHAVEN PRESS

A part of Gale, Cengage Learning

GALE
CENGAGE Learning·

Detroit • New York • San Francisco • New Haven, Conn • Waterville, Maine • London

Elizabeth Des Chenes, *Director, Content Strategy*
Cynthia Sanner, *Publisher*
Douglas Dentino, *Manager, New Product*

LIBRARY OF CONGRESS CATALOGING-IN-PUBLICATION DATA

The aging population / Margaret Haerens, book editor.
   pages cm. -- (Opposing viewpoints)
  Includes bibliographical references and index.
  ISBN 978-0-7377-6943-2 (hardcover) -- ISBN 978-0-7377-6944-9 (pbk.)
  1. Aging. 2. Older people. I. Haerens, Margaret.
  HQ1061.A4298 2014
  305.26--dc23
                                     2013033583

Printed in the United States of America
1 2 3 4 5 6 7 18 17 16 15 14

Contents

Chapter 2: What Are the Social and Legal Issues Related to an Aging Population?

Chapter 3: Is Social Security Viable and Effective for an Aging Population?

Chapter 4: What Medical Challenges Face an Aging Population?

Why Consider Opposing Viewpoints?

"The only way in which a human being can make some approach to knowing the whole of a subject is by hearing what can be said about it by persons of every variety of opinion and studying all modes in which it can be looked at by every character of mind. No wise man ever acquired his wisdom in any mode but this."

John Stuart Mill

In our media-intensive culture it is not difficult to find differing opinions. Thousands of newspapers and magazines and dozens of radio and television talk shows resound with differing points of view. The difficulty lies in deciding which opinion to agree with and which "experts" seem the most credible. The more inundated we become with differing opinions and claims, the more essential it is to hone critical reading and thinking skills to evaluate these ideas. Opposing Viewpoints books address this problem directly by presenting stimulating debates that can be used to enhance and teach these skills. The varied opinions contained in each book examine many different aspects of a single issue. While examining these conveniently edited opposing views, readers can develop critical thinking skills such as the ability to compare and contrast authors' credibility, facts, argumentation styles, use of persuasive techniques, and other stylistic tools. In short, the Opposing Viewpoints Series is an ideal way to attain the higher-level thinking and reading skills so essential in a culture of diverse and contradictory opinions.

In addition to providing a tool for critical thinking, Opposing Viewpoints books challenge readers to question their own strongly held opinions and assumptions. Most people form their opinions on the basis of upbringing, peer pressure, and personal, cultural, or professional bias. By reading carefully balanced opposing views, readers must directly confront new ideas as well as the opinions of those with whom they disagree. This is not to simplistically argue that everyone who reads opposing views will—or should—change his or her opinion. Instead, the series enhances readers' understanding of their own views by encouraging confrontation with opposing ideas. Careful examination of others' views can lead to the readers' understanding of the logical inconsistencies in their own opinions, perspective on why they hold an opinion, and the consideration of the possibility that their opinion requires further evaluation.

Evaluating Other Opinions

To ensure that this type of examination occurs, Opposing Viewpoints books present all types of opinions. Prominent spokespeople on different sides of each issue as well as well-known professionals from many disciplines challenge the reader. An additional goal of the series is to provide a forum for other, less known, or even unpopular viewpoints. The opinion of an ordinary person who has had to make the decision to cut off life support from a terminally ill relative, for example, may be just as valuable and provide just as much insight as a medical ethicist's professional opinion. The editors have two additional purposes in including these less known views. One, the editors encourage readers to respect others' opinions—even when not enhanced by professional credibility. It is only by reading or listening to and objectively evaluating others' ideas that one can determine whether they are worthy of consideration. Two, the inclusion of such viewpoints encourages the important critical thinking skill of objectively evaluating an author's credentials and bias. This evaluation will illuminate an author's reasons for taking a particular stance on an issue and will aid in readers' evaluation of the author's ideas.

It is our hope that these books will give readers a deeper understanding of the issues debated and an appreciation of the complexity of even seemingly simple issues when good and honest people disagree. This awareness is particularly important in a democratic society such as ours in which people enter into public debate to determine the common good. Those with whom one disagrees should not be regarded as enemies but rather as people whose views deserve careful examination and may shed light on one's own.

Thomas Jefferson once said that "difference of opinion leads to inquiry, and inquiry to truth." Jefferson, a broadly educated man, argued that "if a nation expects to be ignorant and free . . . it expects what never was and never will be." As individuals and as a nation, it is imperative that we consider the opinions of others and examine them with skill and discernment. The Opposing Viewpoints Series is intended to help readers achieve this goal.

David L. Bender and Bruno Leone,
Founders

Introduction

"The fact that [baby] boomers are 'coming of age' at a time when life expectancy is lengthening may pose some demographic and economic challenges. But many sociologists and gerontologists believe the generation that refuses to grow up can change—in healthy ways—how Americans think about aging."

Alan Greenblatt,
"Aging Baby Boomers,"
CQ Researcher, October 19, 2007

Born one second after midnight on January 1, 1946, Kathleen Casey-Kirschling is regarded as the nation's first member of the baby boomer generation. Baby boomers are not only America's biggest generational group, they are also one of its most closely studied and celebrated. As Dr. Rhonda L. Randall observes in the *Huffington Post*, "Since making their debut in 1946, baby boomers have been a major force for social change in the United States. Their epic numbers and independent spirit have influenced everything from politics to pop culture, transformed the makeup of the American family and workforce, reshaped societal norms, and created our modern notion of consumerism. Boomers have redefined each phase of life, and they're expected to do the same as they age." On February 8, 2008, a milestone in US history occurred: Ms. Casey-Kirschling received her first Social Security benefits. The baby boom generation had finally reached the age of Social Security eligibility.

According to the US Census, men and women in the baby boom generation were born during the post–World War II baby boom between the years 1946 and 1964. The demographic trend began in 1946, when more babies were born than ever before in American history: 3.4 million, 20 percent more than in 1945. In 1947, another 3.8 million babies were born. The boom continued through 1952, when 3.9 million babies were born. More than 4 million were born every year from 1954 until 1964, when the boom finally tapered off. All in all, there are around 77 million members of the baby boomer generation in the United States, comprising almost 40 percent of the nation's population.

In 2011, Kathleen Casey-Kirschling became the first baby boomer to turn 65 years old, officially launching what some demographers and sociologists have called "the silver tsunami." Over the next several years, nearly 80 million Americans will become eligible for Social Security retirement benefits, more than 10,000 per day on average. They will be turning 65 at a rate of about 8,000 a day. By 2030, nearly 20 percent of the US population will be at least 65 years old. As America's biggest generation ages, it will have profound political, social, and economic effects on the United States and its future.

Many economists contend that the aging of the baby boomer generation will strain the US economy. The recent economic downturn exacerbated worries that many American boomers have not saved enough for retirement or the possibility of long-term medical care. According to some estimates, nearly two-thirds of baby boomers are not financially prepared for the challenges of old age.

The aging of the baby boomer generation will have a major impact on government entitlement programs, as older Americans apply for Medicare and Social Security benefits. As reporter Jim Tankersley observes in *The Atlantic*, the boomers will receive better benefits than earlier generations. "Boomers will be the first generation of retirees to fully enjoy the Medicare prescription drug benefit; because Social Security payouts rise faster than price inflation, they will draw more-generous retirement benefits than their parents did, in real terms—at their children's expense," he notes. "The Urban Institute estimated last year that a couple retiring in 2011, having both earned average wages, will accrue about $200,000 more in Medicare and Social Security benefits over their lifetimes than they paid in taxes to support those programs."

Because they have to serve growing numbers of American seniors, the government will have to find a way to maintain funding for such programs. In 1975 Social Security, Medicare and Medicaid made up 25 percent of federal spending. Today they add up to about 40 percent. By 2025, these programs will comprise about half of all federal outlays.

The role and future of Social Security and Medicare have become divisive political issues. One of the most contentious political issues in recent years have been proposals to privatize Social Security: some politicians and policy makers want to reduce the government's role in subsidizing and administering the program, instead turning it over to private companies. Critics of such reforms view the privatization proposal as an attempt to eventually eliminate the program and enrich business interests at the expense of seniors. Supporters argue that private companies can do a more efficient job in administering Social Security and allows seniors to have more input in their financial decisions.

In spite of political squabbles on how to administer the program and questions about its long-term financial viability, it is clear from a wide range of public opinion polls that the American public strongly supports Social Security, across party and demographic lines. A 2013 National Academy of Social Insurance (NASI) and Rockefeller Foundation poll found that nearly nine in ten Americans (88 percent) believe that Social Security is more essential than ever in light of the recent economic crisis. In addition, three-quarters of Americans say it is critical to preserve Social Security even if it means that working Americans have to pay higher taxes to do so. These polls show that Americans recognize that Social Security is vital to the economic security of older Americans. That's why Social Security is called "the third rail of politics" and political proposals to reform it have derailed the careers of many American policy makers.

Baby boomers already have a major influence on many social issues. Polls show that they are more tolerant than earlier generations of same-sex marriage, civil unions, premarital sex, divorce, and raising children outside the boundaries of traditional family structures. More and more boomers use social media and spend significant time online watching video and surfing the Internet.

In assessing the influence of the baby boom generation, the AARP notes in its December 2010 report "Approaching 65: A Survey of Baby Boomers Turning 65 Years Old" that the boomers have left an indelible mark on modern American life. "The impact of the baby boom generation and of specific baby boomers cannot be underestimated," the report suggests. "In every aspect of American life, from entertainment to politics or to sport, baby boomers are the prime movers. The last three US presidents have been boomers as are a majority of senators and the members of the House of Representatives. One only needs to look at the number of remade television programs and movies from the '60s and '70s to see how entertainment decisions are being made by boomers or for boomers."

The authors of the viewpoints included in *Opposing Viewpoints: The Aging Population* explore the economic, social, and political consequences of an aging population in the following chapters: What Are the Economic Consequences of an Aging Population?, What Are the Social and Legal Issues Related to an Aging Population?, Is Social Security Viable and Effective for an Aging Population?, and What Medical Challenges Face an Aging Population? The information found in this volume should provide insight into issues facing the United States as it ages, including the rising rates of drug addiction and substance abuse; epidemics of dementia and Alzheimer's disease; the need for long-term care and economic stability into old age; the problems of age discrimination and aging drivers; and the role of seniors in the national economy.

What Are the Economic Consequences of an Aging Population?

Chapter Preface

The origins of the US Medicare program can be traced back to President Harry Truman's effort to pass universal health care for all Americans in 1945. In November of that year, he sent a special message to the US Congress outlining the need for a national health care program. "Millions of our citizens do not now have a full measure of opportunity to achieve and enjoy good health," the message read. "Millions do not now have protection or security against the economic effects of sickness. The time has arrived for action to help them attain that opportunity and that protection." Although the need was great—millions of Americans suffered from a lack of affordable health care in those years—Truman's campaign to create a national health care program ultimately failed.

In 1960 the US Congress passed the Kerr-Mills Act, which was the first attempt to provide subsidized health care for the elderly. Under the Medical Assistance for the Aged (MAA) program, the federal government gave money to the states to help provide health care for the elderly, especially in the South. Only thirty-two states, however, adopted it. Health care remained out of reach for many elderly Americans: only half of Americans over the age of 65 had healthcare insurance; of those who did had poor coverage.

It was President Lyndon B. Johnson who finally got a national health care program for seniors into law. In 1965 the US Congress passed Medicare under the Social Security Act, which provided health insurance to more than 18 million Americans age 65 and older, regardless of income level or medical history. At the signing of the bill, President Johnson celebrated with the president who had first pushed the idea of national health care, Harry Truman.

"No longer will older Americans be denied the healing miracle of modern medicine," Johnson exclaimed at the signing ceremony on July 30, 1965. "No longer will illness crush and destroy the savings that they have so carefully put away over a lifetime so that they might enjoy dignity in their later years. No longer will young families see their own incomes, and their own hopes, eaten away simply because they are carrying out their deep moral obligations to their parents, and to their uncles, and their aunts. And no longer will this Nation refuse the hand of justice to those who have given a lifetime of service and wisdom and labor to the progress of this progressive country."

Since Medicare's implementation, there have been several reforms of the program. In 1972 Medicare was expanded to include benefits for speech, physical, and chiropractic therapy; extend eligibility to younger Americans with permanent disabilities; and provide coverage through health maintenance organizations (HMOs). In 1982 hospice benefits were added to Medicare. A year later, a new payment program was implemented to control rising health care costs.

In 1997 legislation, the US Congress expanded the role of private health care plans by creating Medicare+Choice, now called Medicare Advantage, a health insurance program run by a private health insurance company. The Medicare Modernization Act of 2003 added a controversial prescription drug benefit, known as Part D, delivered only through private insurance plans. The Affordable Care Act (ACA) was passed in 2010, providing preventive health services, like annual physicals, for seniors. The ACA also aims to make Medicare more efficient, reduce health care costs, and improve the program's solvency.

The growing number of American seniors on Medicare is explored in the following chapter, which investigates the economic consequences of an aging population. Other viewpoints in the chapter examine the impact of aging demographics on economic growth, national security, and geopolitical challenges the United States faces in the twenty-first century.

| "*Global aging will be a potent force for the continuation of American military and economic dominance.*"

Global Aging Poses Long-Term Economic, Geopolitical, and National Security Challenges

Mark L. Haas

Mark L. Haas is an author, educator, and expert on foreign policy. In the following viewpoint, he examines the long-term implications of aging population on global economics, politics, and security. Haas finds that global aging will lead to continued US economic and military dominance, because many governments will be forced to pay massive amounts of money to care for their elderly populations instead of devoting the resources needed to compete in the global arena. The United States has a demographic advantage, he says, because it has higher fertility and immigration rates than other developed nations and is better positioned to meet the significant challenges that an aging population poses. Although China is a rising economic power, Haas predicts it will be hard hit by a major demographic crisis in the coming years and will see its economic and political power wane.

As you read, consider the following questions:

1. According to Haas, by how much is Russia's population decreasing every year?

2. How much are Japan's and Russia's working-age populations expected to shrink by 2050, according to Haas?

3. According to the Congressional Budget Office, how much will the United States spend on the elderly by 2015?

Last year [2007], Sergei Morozov, the governor of the Ulyanovsk region of central Russia, offered prizes to couples who agreed to take advantage of a "family contact day" and wound up producing babies nine months later, on June 12, Russia's national day. It was the third year running that Ulyanovsk had declared a "sex day" and offered prizes for babies born, according to the BBC. The 2007 grand prize (for conceptions in 2006, of course) was a sport utility vehicle.

Demographic Crises

The Ulyanovsk initiative is just a part of Russia's efforts to fight a looming demographic crisis that hovers over much of the world. Simply put, the world's great powers are growing old. Steep declines in birthrates over the last century and major increases in life expectancies have caused the populations of Britain, China, France, Germany, Japan, Russia and the United States to age at a substantial rate. In Russia, declining birthrates and other factors are not just aging the society but actually shrinking the country's population.

This phenomenon will have critical effects on America's international-security interests in coming decades. Most important, global aging will be a potent force for the continuation of American military and economic dominance. Aging populations are likely to result in the slowdown of states' economic growth at the same time that governments face pressure to pay for massive new expenditures for elderly care. This double economic dilemma will create such an austere fiscal environment that the other great powers will lack the resources necessary to overtake the United States' huge power lead. This analysis applies even to China, which most analysts point to as America's most likely future rival. China's aging problem will be particularly dramatic over the next 40 years, which will make it difficult for it to challenge American international supremacy.

Meanwhile, America also seems likely to face fewer threats from terrorism based in Islamic countries. If current demographic trends continue, many Islamic states—now in the throes of "youth bulges"—will be aging as societies in coming decades. As active and disaffected young people have aged in other parts of the world, they have become a source of political stability and economic development. There is reason to believe this pattern will hold in Iraq, Pakistan, Saudi Arabia and other Muslim states as their youth slip into middle age.

Although the United States is also growing older, it is doing so to a lesser extent and less quickly than the other great powers. Consequently, the costs created by aging will be significantly lower for the U.S. than for potential competitors. Global aging is therefore likely not only to extend U.S. dominance (because the other major powers will lack the resources necessary to overtake the United States' economic and military power lead) but also to deepen it as these other states are likely to fall even farther behind the United States. By inhibiting the other powers from challenging American primacy, global aging increases the odds in favor of continued peaceful relations among these states. *Pax Americana* is therefore likely to extend well into the 21st century.

Although the United States is in better demographic shape than the other great powers, it, too, will confront massive new costs created by an aging population. The U.S. will be more secure from great-power rivalry than it is today, but it (and its allies) will be less able to realize other key international objectives, including preventing the proliferation of weapons of mass destruction, funding nation building and engaging in humanitarian interventions, among the many costly conflict-resolution and prevention efforts it now undertakes. To protect America's future international interests, it is vital that the country's current leaders adopt policies designed to strengthen its demographic advantages. In the future, America's ability to pay to care for its elderly citizens will become a matter not just of compassion but of national security.

Something New Under the Sun

The scope of the aging process in the great powers—a result of historically low fertility rates and expanding life expectancies—is unprecedented. By 2050, at least 20 percent of the citizens in Britain, China, France, Germany, Japan, Russia and the U.S. will be over 65, according to United Nations projections. In Japan, more than one of every three people will be over this age. In 2050, China will have more than 329 million people over 65, a total approximately equal to the entire current populations of France, Germany, Japan and the United Kingdom combined. As aging progresses over the next half-century, the populations in Germany, Japan and Russia are expected to shrink significantly. Russia's population is already decreasing by nearly 700,000 people per year, and Japan, too, is experiencing population decline. Russia's aging problem is so severe that, in 2006, *The New York Times* quoted President Vladimir Putin calling demography "Russia's most acute problem today."

The aging of the world's great powers is also happening quickly. It took France 115 years for the size of its 65-and-over age group to double from 7 to 14 percent of its population. The U.S. took 69 years to do so. China will experience this transformation in 27 years, or roughly one generation. China, in fact, will age at a pace and extent scarcely before witnessed in human history.

It is worth stressing that the predictions for global aging are very unlikely to be wrong. The reason for this certainty is simple: The elderly of the future are already born. Consequently, absent some global natural disaster, disease pandemic or other worldwide calamity (all extremely rare historically), the number of people in the world who are over 65 will increase dramatically in coming decades. Only major increases in immigration rates or fertility levels will prevent this inevitable rise in the number of elderly from resulting in significant increases in median ages in these states.

Such outcomes are unlikely. Over the next 50 years, immigration rates in the great powers would have to be orders of magnitude higher than historical levels to prevent population aging. Not only do the sheer numbers work against such an outcome, but some countries are becoming more hostile to immigration, despite its benefits for social aging. Both Japan and Russia passed laws in 2006 that will restrict immigration to these states, and right-wing parties have been on the rise across Europe since the 1990s, spurred largely by hostility toward immigrants.

Significant increases in fertility are also unlikely. Such an outcome would require a reversal of a centuries-long trend in the industrialized world, and one that has existed in many states despite the existence of pro-fertility governmental policies (perhaps the most direct of these being Russia's "sex days").

Aging in the most powerful actors in the international system is, in short, a virtual inevitability.

The Costs of Growing Old

In its most basic formulation, a state's gross domestic product is a product of the number of workers and overall productivity. When a country's work force shrinks as more people enter retirement than enter the labor market, so, too, will its GDP [gross domestic product, a country's measure of economic output], unless productivity levels rise sufficiently to compensate for the loss. Japan's and Russia's working-age populations (ages 15 to 64) are expected to shrink by 34 percent by 2050, Germany's by 20 percent, France's by 6 percent and China's by 3 percent. To prevent these work force reductions from translating into overall GDP decline, states' productivity must increase proportionally. Although productivity will likely increase in most industrialized countries, work force contraction will still act as a substantial brake on economic growth in coming decades.

We are already witnessing this dynamic. Even though China is the youngest of the great powers, it is experiencing labor shortages that are threatening economic growth. These shortages are due in large part to the aging of China and reductions in the number of 15- to 35-year-olds there. Experts predict that shrinkage in China's working-age population will result in a loss of 1 percent per year from this state's GDP growth by the 2020s. The economic forecasts are even more dire for France, Germany and Japan, where massively contracting labor forces could result in *overall* annual GDP growth of roughly 1 percent in coming decades.

Significant societal aging may also limit productivity growth. The elderly are likely to be more conservative with their investments than younger people. The more risk averse a society's investment portfolio is, the less entrepreneurship will be funded and, thus, the lower the gains in productivity. National savings rates may also shrink in aging states as seniors spend down their savings. The Japanese government has already reported that national savings rates are down substantially due to social aging. Reduced savings may lead to rising interest rates and ultimately to reduced rates of productivity increases.

Other Consequences of an Aging Population

An even more important economic effect of societal aging is the strain that it places on governmental resources. All governments in the industrialized world have made commitments to pay for substantial portions of the retirement and health care costs of their elderly citizens. Social aging increases these obligations in two principal respects. First, the older a society is, the greater the number of retirees and senior citizens for which a particular government is responsible. Second, the elderly, on average, require significantly more resources than working-age adults. Studies have shown that seniors use three to five times more medical care than younger people, for example.

The pension systems across the industrialized world will be particularly taxing on governments' fiscal policies. The public pensions in all of the great powers are "pay as you go," meaning that current workers are taxed to support current retirees. This type of system does not place a significant strain on a state's economy as long as relatively high numbers of workers contribute to the system in relation to retirees. This will not be the case for much longer across the industrial world, and, in some cases, it is not true even today. France, Germany, Japan and Britain have roughly only four working-age adults per senior citizen. By 2050, only America among the great powers will have more than three working-age adults per elderly person.

The projected increases in governmental spending for the elderly in coming decades are sobering. Annual public pension and health care benefits to the elderly as a percentage of GDP are predicted to rise in 2040 by 15 percent in Japan (to an overall percentage of 27); by 13 percent in France (to an overall percentage of 29); by 11 percent in the United States (to an overall percentage of 20); by 10 percent in Germany (to an overall percentage of 26); and by 6 percent in Britain (to an overall percentage of 18).

These costs will be an increase of hundreds of billions of dollars to governments' annual expenditures for many decades. To give some perspective on their magnitude, consider the following: Roughly 35 years from now, the annual amount of money that the great powers will have to spend on elderly care is going to increase by many times what these states currently spend on their militaries, even after adjusting for inflation. By 2040, Germany will have to increase its annual spending on elderly care by more than seven times what it currently spends on defense. France will have to spend more than five times as much and Japan more than 15 times as much.

Pax Americana Geriatrica

Population aging in the great powers will help prolong U.S. power dominance in the 21st century for three primary reasons. First, the massive costs created by aging populations, especially in combination with probable slowdowns in economic growth, will inhibit other major powers from significantly increasing military expenditures; these factors are even likely to push many of these states to reduce military spending from current levels. Second, with aging populations and shrinking work forces, other great powers will be forced to decide whether to spend increasing percentages of their defense budgets on personnel costs and military pensions, at the expense of the most technologically sophisticated weaponry. The third factor reinforces both of the previous points: Although the U.S. population is aging, it is doing so to a lesser extent and less quickly than those of the other great powers. The pressures pushing for the crowding out of military spending in favor of elderly care and the increasing substitution of labor for capital within defense budgets will be considerably smaller for the U.S. than for potential great-power competitors. By inhibiting the other powers from challenging America's huge power lead, global aging will increase the likelihood of continued peaceful relations among these states.

We are, in fact, already witnessing in some states the crowding out of military spending for elderly care. Japan reduced military spending in the 2005 and 2006 budgets explic-

The Asian Century

Those who predict a coming Asian Century have not come to terms with the region's approaching era of hyper-aging. Japan, whose "lost decade" began just as its labor force started to shrink in the late 1980s, now appears to be not an exception, but a vanguard of Asian demographics. South Korea and Taiwan, with some of the lowest birth rates of any major country, will be losing population within 15 years. Singapore's government is so worried about its birth dearth that it not only offers new mothers a "baby bonus" of up to about $3,000 each for the first or second child and about $4,500 for a third or fourth child, paid maternity leave, and other enticements to have children, it has even started sponsoring speed-dating events.

Phillip Longman, "Think Again: Global Aging,"
Foreign Policy, November 2010. www.foreignpolicy.com.

itly to pay for costs created by its rapidly aging population. The Japanese government has stated that over the next decade, general expenditures will have to be cut by 25 to 30 percent to address this problem. Similar pressure for cuts in defense spending to finance elderly-care costs is building in France and Germany.

China's Rapidly Aging Society

The decision to cut military spending to pay elderly-care costs is likely to repeat itself in the state that is aging faster than any of the great powers: China. Rising longevity in China and the "one-child policy," which has helped lower dramatically China's fertility levels, have made China a rapidly aging society. By 2050, according to the U.N. [United Nations], China's median age is predicted to be nearly 45, one of the oldest in the world. (The oldest country in the world today, Japan, has a median age of just under 43). The ratio of working-age adults to elderly will shrink from just under 10 in 2000 to 2.5 by 2050. China today has roughly 100 million citizens over the age of 65. This number will double in 20 years. Roughly 30 years from now, it is expected to triple.

Despite the effects of the one-child policy on China's median age, China's leaders are unlikely to repeal it in the near future. *The New York Times* reports that the Chinese government significantly increased the fines this year for wealthy couples who violate the law and have more than one child. Although some Chinese officials talk about reconsidering this law, any changes that do occur will most likely be incremental. The longer the one-child policy stays in effect, the more quickly China will age.

China is particularly unprepared to pay for the costs of its rapidly aging population. China's elderly have very little savings. Nearly 80 percent of Chinese urban households with individuals aged 55 and over today have less than one year of income saved, and only 5 percent have more than two years of income in savings, according to Center for Strategic and International Studies and Asian Development Bank research. The Chinese government has also failed to set aside over the decades sufficient money to pay for elderly-care costs. Three-quarters of all Chinese workers are without any pension coverage, yet independent estimates have found a potential shortfall between China's governmental obligations to the elderly and saved assets to be as much as 150 percent of its GDP.

China will not be able to "grow" its way out of this dilemma. Despite China's very high levels of economic growth since the 1990s, it will become the first country to grow old before becoming an advanced industrial state. Even if China's economy continues to grow in coming decades at rates similar to those it has experienced in recent years, by 2035, its median age will reach the levels of France, Germany and Japan today but at GDP-per-capita levels significantly lower than these states currently possess.

Growing the Welfare State in China

China has traditionally relied on the family unit to provide for elderly care in lieu of adequate public and private resources. But as *The New York Times* has noted, increasing rates of divorce, urbanization (and related migration) and female work force participation will place significant strain on this tradition. Decreasing family size will prove especially problematic for preserving elderly welfare within the context of the family. Demographers refer to a rapidly growing "4-2-1" phenomenon in China, in which one child is responsible for caring for two parents and four grandparents.

Within 15 years, China's leaders will be faced with a difficult choice: Allow growing levels of poverty within an exploding elderly population, or provide the resources necessary to avoid this situation. The Chinese government's assumption since 2000 of unfunded pension liabilities of state-owned enterprises reveals the political and moral pressure working for the latter outcome. This pressure to significantly expand and deepen China's welfare system will only grow as its aging crisis becomes increasingly acute in the decades to come. In this context, the crowding out of military and other discretionary expenditures will be likely, to the great benefit of America's relative power position.

Aging and the Effect on the Military

Aging is also likely to push militaries to spend more on personnel and less on other areas, including weapons development and procurement. This is important because no nation will be able to challenge U.S. military dominance without the ability to wage highly technologically sophisticated warfare. When states are forced to spend more of their military budgets on personnel than research, development and weapons procurement, the odds of continued U.S. military primacy increase substantially.

The oldest of the great powers are already devoting significantly more resources to military personnel than weapons purchases and research. Over the last 10 years, both France and Germany have dedicated nearly 60 percent of their military budgets to personnel. Germany spends nearly four times as much on personnel as weapons procurement; France, Japan and Russia roughly 2.5 times more. The U.S., in contrast, dedicates only 1.15 times more money to personnel than weapons purchases.

Population aging is a key cause of increasing military personnel costs for two main reasons. First, as societies age, more people exit the work force than enter it. Increasing numbers of retirees in relation to new workers are likely to create labor shortages relative to previous levels of employment. The result will be increased competition among businesses and organizations—including the military—to hire workers. Consequently, if states' militaries want to be able to attract and keep the best employees in vital areas of operation—especially those in high-tech fields who usually have the most employment options and can command high salaries in the private sector—they are going to have to pay more to do so. If militaries do not increase their outlays for personnel, their effectiveness will diminish. A 2006 report endorsed by EU defense ministers made precisely these points, stating that the aging of Europe's people will "inevitably" lead to rising military personnel per capita costs if European forces are to remain effective.

Similarly, to keep military salaries on par with wages in its expanding economy, China—even though its armed forces are conscripted—has had to raise military wages sharply in recent years. According to the Chinese government, growing personnel expenses are the most important factor behind the growth of China's defense budget in the last decade.

The great powers' pension obligations to retired military personnel are also considerable. Russia spends significantly more on military retirees than on either weapons procurement or military research and development, according to its 2006 defense budget.

Pensions for military retirees are not one-time costs but go on for decades, doing nothing to increase states' power-projection capabilities. Every dollar spent on retirees is one less dollar that can be spent on weapons, research or active personnel. Consequently, every dollar spent in this area by the other great powers increases the likelihood of continued U.S. primacy.

U.S. Aging: Bad, but Better Than the Rest

At a gala event held at the National Press Club in Washington, D.C., on Oct. 15, 2007, Kathleen Casey-Kirschling, who was born one second after midnight on Jan. 1, 1946, became the first baby boomer to file for Social Security. Over the next 20 years, 76 million Americans from the age cohort born between 1946 and 1964 will join her.

The costs created by America's aging population are staggering. The Congressional Budget Office projects that by 2015, spending on the elderly will total almost $1.8 trillion, nearly half of the anticipated federal budget. Health care costs, in particular, are the United States' biggest problem regarding societal aging. The United States spends more than twice as much per capita in this area than any other industrial great power (though it ranks 48th in the world in life expectancy). According to conservative estimates—absent reforms—the costs of Medicare alone will be at least $2.6 trillion in 2050, after adjusting for inflation, which is roughly the size of the current U.S. federal budget.

Despite these expected cost increases, the United States is in significantly better shape to address the challenges created by its aging population than the other powers. The U.S. is the youngest of all the G-8 nations. Because it has the highest fertility and immigration rates of these countries, it will maintain, even strengthen, this position in coming decades. In 2050, the United States' median age will be the lowest of any of the great powers, in most cases by a substantial extent. (China's median age will surpass the United States' by 2020.) Perhaps most important, while the working-age populations in all the other great powers are predicted by 2050 to either decline (China, France, Germany, Japan and Russia) or increase modestly (Britain), this demographic group is expected to increase by 31 percent in the U.S.

The U.S. in a Power Position

The United States' relatively youthful demographics will help greatly with the fiscal challenges created by aging. The growing U.S. labor force over the next 50 years will contribute to an expanding economy, thereby providing the government with additional revenue without it having to increase taxes, borrow more money or cut other spending. In addition, the United States has a relatively well-funded pension system (especially in relation to China, France, Germany and Russia); its public welfare commitments to the elderly are relatively modest compared with those of other industrialized powers; its citizens work many more hours per year and significantly later in life than the average individual in the other powers; and its tax burden is low compared with those of other powers.

American expectations are also comparatively favorable. In a 2008 Harris Interactive poll of citizens in the United States, Britain, France, Germany, Italy and Spain, Americans had the highest predictions of when they would retire (67.2 years old) and the lowest expectations—by far—regarding governmental support of their retirement. (Only 27 percent of Americans believed that the national government should bear most of their retirement costs; this percentage ranged from 45 to 72 in

European countries.) These expectations reveal that U.S. citizens are much more amenable to entitlement reforms and benefit cuts than are most Europeans.

Again, the preceding facts do not mean that the U.S. will escape the fiscal burdens created by aging or that this phenomenon will not create negative ramifications for U.S. security. Rather, as burdensome as the public costs of aging will be for the United States, the public benefits owed to U.S. seniors as a percentage of GDP will likely remain substantially lower than in most of the other great powers. Moreover, the U.S. will be better positioned to pay for these costs than the other major actors. Global aging will therefore be a powerful force for the continuation of the relative power dominance of the United States.

"As population aging is elevated to the global agenda, the countries that capitalize on the increasing percentage of older adults, and are able to increasingly facilitate their meaningful contributions, will secure a strategic and competitive advantage in the years to come."

An Aging Population Can Drive Economic Growth

Robert D. Hormats

Robert D. Hormats is the US under secretary of state for economic growth, energy, and the environment. In the following viewpoint, he suggests that global aging presents both challenges and opportunities for countries around the world. Hormats underscores the importance of creating opportunities to enable aging populations to continue to contribute economically and remain productive citizens. Governments should craft policies to improve this continued productivity, including innovations in medicine and education. He argues that countries that are successful in capitalizing on their aging populations will have a competitive advantage in the twenty-first century.

Robert D. Hormats, "The Aging Population: Economic Growth and Global Competitiveness," *DipNote: U.S. Department of State Official Blog*, February 13, 2012. http://blogs.state.gov.

As you read, consider the following questions:

1. How many US baby boomers does Hormats estimate are beginning to transition into retirement?

2. According to the author, how many people worldwide will be over the age of 60 by 2050?

3. What did the European Union designate 2012?

On Tuesday, February 14, [2012,] the Council on Foreign Relations is holding a meeting on the "The U.S. Aging Population as an Economic Growth Driver for Global Competitiveness." The event is timely. Standard & Poor's reports that "No other force is likely to shape the future of national economic health, public finances and policy-making as the irreversible rate at which the world's population is aging."

Hence, it's vital that we create opportunities to enable older persons to contribute to their economies and communities in increasingly effective and productive ways. This will require new policies and innovations that promote healthy aging, including advances in medicine, continued learning, and cultural norms regarding aging. As population aging is elevated to the global agenda, the countries that capitalize on the increasing percentage of older adults, and are able to increasingly facilitate their meaningful contributions, will secure a strategic and competitive advantage in the years to come.

The Challenges and Opportunities of an Aging Population

Consider the demographic facts: In the United States, 77 million Baby Boomers—born from 1946 through 1964—are beginning to transition into retirement. In addition to increasing the strain on government-sponsored programs like Medicare, Medicaid, and Social Security, the retirement of this large group of Americans could also create significant losses in productivity as well as specialized skills upon which many of our companies depend.

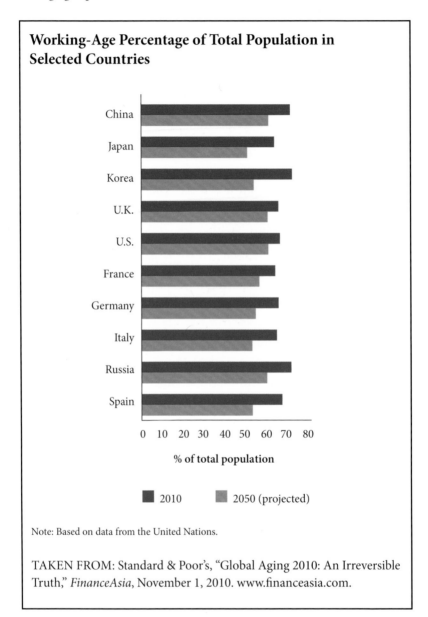

Working-Age Percentage of Total Population in Selected Countries

% of total population

■ 2010   ■ 2050 (projected)

Note: Based on data from the United Nations.

TAKEN FROM: Standard & Poor's, "Global Aging 2010: An Irreversible Truth," *FinanceAsia*, November 1, 2010. www.financeasia.com.

The United States is not alone in the challenge and opportunity of population aging. By 2050, more than two billion people worldwide will be over the age of 60. By then, for the first time in human history, more people will be over the age of 60 than under 15. Life-spans have increased an incredible three decades in the past one hundred years and disability rates have been declining. The science of health promotion and risk factor reduction, coupled with advancements in medicine, have made it possible for a large percentage of the population to live out their lives in functional and productive ways. Longevity and health, however, are only part of the equation. As more people worldwide enter their traditional retirement years, the dependency ratio (i.e., the number of retirees per worker) will skyrocket requiring prudent review of twentieth century retirement models.

Providing opportunities for continued contribution by an aging population is an economic imperative in a growing number of countries, both developing and developed nations. This is a new challenge for developing country governments, especially in Latin America and Asia, which over the past few decades have experienced a significant drop in fertility and death rates. That's why the Asia-Pacific Economic Cooperation (APEC) has declared economic success to be a function of the health and productivity of APEC's Member Economies' aging populations. This declaration is supported by other global organizations also working to turn aging into an opportunity. Indeed, the European Union has launched 2012 as its year of Active and Healthy Aging. And the World Health Organization (WHO) has begun an Age-Friendly Cities Program and is dedicating 2012 World Health Day to aging populations.

Equally significant is the global health community's new focus on age-related health challenges, called non communicable diseases (NCDs), such as cardiovascular and respiratory diseases, cancer and diabetes. A WHO Resolution calling on governments to "strengthen NCD policies to promote active aging" will be at the center of this year's World Health Assembly in May. This work is an important sign that aging is now beginning to occupy a critical and rightful place on the international agenda.

A Positive Driver of Growth

We need a focused, society-wide effort to transform our vision of aging from a time of dependency to a time of continued growth, contribution, and social and economic participation. Older adults have a wealth of experience and much to contribute. We need a sea-change not just in policies, but in attitudes about what it means to grow old. We must break the stereotype that to be old is to be inactive or dependent, and in so doing turn "population aging" into the century's greatest achievement.

Collaborating with our private sector and global partners is a path to sharing strategies and solutions to the truly global phenomenon of population aging. On the government side, an important step will be to broaden the base of collaboration on aging populations to include not only health, but also economic, finance and trade portfolios. Working together, we can turn the longevity bequeathed us from the twentieth century into a positive driver of growth, contribution and economic activity in the twenty-first.

> "A true retirement crisis is looming in the U.S., but politicians, obsessed with Social Security projections decades into the future, are disinclined to address it."

An Aging Population Will Cause Economic Stagnation and a Rise in Poverty

Eric Laursen

Eric Laursen is an author and journalist. In the following viewpoint, he outlines the retirement crisis looming in the United States. Laursen maintains that while politicians in Washington are appointing presidential commissions bent on cutting Social Security and Medicaid benefits for seniors, the financial resources that older people thought they could depend on in their retirement are disappearing. As a result, shocking numbers of retired Americans live in poverty and face daunting economic challenges. One of the biggest challenges is wage stagnation, which has depressed Social Security's revenue stream for years. The effects of the economic downturn—especially the employment crisis—has also had terrible consequences for Americans nearing retirement. *Laursen contends that the media has largely abdicated its role to report on the issue, instead focusing on the need to reform entitlements and reflecting Washington groupthink.*

As you read, consider the following questions:

1. According to the US Census Bureau, what percentage of Americans over 65 live in poverty?

2. At what age does Laursen say Americans can collect Social Security benefits?

3. According to the US Census Bureau, what percentage of American households received Social Security, subsidized housing, unemployment insurance, or other government benefits?

The astounding, and potentially tragic, aspect of Washington's three-plus-decade Social Security debate is that it carries on with little regard to the challenges facing the program's participants. Politicians on the right and center-right feel free to decry resistance to even "modest cuts" in Social Security benefits while ignoring the vulnerability of seniors who are living the effects of reductions already mandated in the program's last major overhaul, in 1983.

Alarming New Statistics

But the situation for seniors—and future retirees—is becoming alarming. A new, supplemental poverty measure introduced by the Census Bureau last November [2011] nearly doubled the official estimate of Americans over 65 living in poverty, to 15.9%, mainly due to medical costs not counted in the official numbers. More than 34% were either poor or near-poor—defined as having family income less than twice the poverty line. Half of all retirement-age persons who were no longer working—that is, who were receiving Social Security—had total yearly income of less than $16,140—only a fraction more than the federal minimum wage.

© Brian Fray/CartoonStock.com.

Even small reductions in benefits, or slower growth over a period of years, could tip many of these people into poverty. Countless others, who once believed their personal savings, 401(k)s, employer-sponsored pensions, or the equity in their homes made their retirements secure, are finding out that this isn't the case either. Meanwhile, the White House, Republicans, and centrist Democrats are reportedly negotiating a Grand Bargain built on the deficit-cutting Bowles-Simpson [a 2010 presidential commission tasked with lowering the US deficit] proposals, which would include deep reductions to Social Security. And state and local governments are scrounging for ways to cut back the rest of the safety net for seniors—targeting Medicaid funds for nursing homes and home health care, housing subsidies, and other benefits.

A true retirement crisis is looming in the U.S., but politicians, obsessed with Social Security projections decades into the future, are disinclined to address it. Financially vulnerable older workers will be affected almost as soon as they retire; workers in their 20s, 30s, and 40s today will be hit much harder.

The Social Security "deficit"—the amount by which annual old-age and Disability Insurance benefits are expected to exceed revenues—was projected in 2011 to total about $6.5 trillion over the next 75 years. But for all the political attention focused on it, the economic impact of that shortfall will be quite moderate, equaling just .7% of GDP [gross domestic product, a country's measure of economic output]. Even the Baby Boom retirement wave wouldn't make a very big dent in the economy, according to the Social Security trustees, whose 2011 Annual Report estimated that the annual cost of benefits will rise gradually to 6.2% of GDP by 2035, decline to about 6% by 2050, then stabilize at about that level.

The Retirement Income Deficit

By contrast, the U.S. faces a "retirement income deficit" of $6.6 trillion—larger than Social Security's projected 75-year shortfall and five times the size of the current-year federal deficit. The Retirement Income Deficit is a new measure unveiled in fall 2010 by the Center for Retirement Research at Boston College. It lumps together all the resources that Americans in their peak earning years will have to retire on: Social Security and pension benefits, retirement savings, home equity, and other assets. It calculates the income people will need in retirement, based on tax scenarios as well as the income replacement targets that Americans at different income levels will likely need to meet.

Social Security and Medicare are perhaps the only ingredients in the Retirement Income Deficit calculation that the elderly can still rely upon. Nearly two-thirds depend on Social Security for more than half their income, and roughly one in five for all of it. Without Social Security, nearly half of Americans over 65 would be living in poverty. If anything, dependence on Social Security has [been] increasing since the latest economic slump, thanks to the collapsed housing market, the recession, decades of stagnating wages, and the disintegration of other elements of the social safety net, among other factors.

Not that it's a lot to lean on. Social Security only replaces 37% of the average worker's pre-retirement income at 65. More than 95% of recipients get less than $2,000 a month from the program. Women average less than $12,000 a year in benefits, compared to $14,000 for retirees overall, thanks to the gender pay gap—partially explaining why 75% of old people living in poverty in the U.S. are women. While this seems to merit little discussion in deficit-obsessed Washington or on Wall Street, it draws an alarming picture for anyone familiar with what's happening in the rest of the country, where a Gallup poll found 90% of people aged 44 to 75 agreeing that the country faces a retirement crisis.

Problems with Social Security

Even before the economic slump, however, there were reasons to worry about the erosion of Social Security.

First was the age at which retirees can begin collecting full benefits—which, under the 1983 changes, is scheduled to rise gradually from 65 to 67 for those born in 1938 or later. Second are the premiums for Medicare Parts B and D, which the government deducts straight from recipients' Social Security checks, and are expected to go up sharply. Third, seniors with moderate incomes can expect the tax rate on their Social Security payments to rise because the ceilings built into the tax code aren't inflation-indexed.

The fourth and perhaps largest problem is wage stagnation. Rising wages alone don't ensure Social Security's solvency. While higher wages boost payroll taxes, they also raise benefits. But the fact remains that Social Security can't pay benefits without an adequate revenue stream to cover benefits over time.

Wage stagnation has been depressing payroll taxes for many years—real hourly wages in 2010 were at about 1974 levels—and the economic crisis exacerbates the problem. Payroll tax revenues declined by 1.13-percentage-points of payroll in 2010—more than $60 billion—from what the trustees projected in 2009, "due to a deeper recession and slower recovery than had been expected."

Unless Americans get a raise, their prospects—and Social Security's—will only worsen, because other resources that working people once thought would carry them through retirement—and thus relieve the pressure on Social Security—are disappearing.

The crisis is approaching fastest for older workers. A poll of Americans aged 47 to 65, by the Associated Press and LifeGoesStrong.com, found that almost three-quarters expect to work after reaching retirement age. Getting work won't be easy, however. Labor Department statistics show that 17.4% of Americans nearing retirement—those between 55 and 65—either are unemployed or have been looking for work so long that they have given up. More than 60% of those over 50, in a Rutgers University survey, say they don't expect to hold another full-time position in their field.

The nature of programs for the elderly, meanwhile, is changing. Far from easing into retirement, nearly half of all workers aged 58 and older hold physically demanding jobs that put them at risk of becoming disabled. Disability Insurance has become a sort of early-early retirement plan for some workers, although a stingy one—it pays an average of only $1,064 a month. The ranks of "disability retirees" are bound to grow, too, swelled by the aging baby boomers.

Health Care Issues

One of their biggest budgets worries will be health care. Medicare co-pays only cover between 20% and 45% of the cost of many outpatient treatment programs and services. The average cost of a private room in a nursing home tops $75,000 a year, and government doesn't provide assistance unless the patient is financially tapped out. Medigap insurance policies help, but the premiums run $150 to $250 a month per person, and many insurance companies are getting out of covering long-term care. It was welcome news last October [2011] when Social Security announced that seniors would be getting their first cost-of-living raises in two years in 2012—a healthy boost of 3.6%. For retirees who were lower-income earners, however, Medicare Part B premiums will slice about 43% off the increase, deducted before their Social Security checks are even printed.

Yet, according to the Center for Retirement Research, some two-thirds of Americans are expected to require long-term care at some point during their retirement, whether at home or in nursing facilities. One study projects that spending on long-term care for the elderly will triple by 2040. Alzheimer's Disease is increasing among the very old. Medicare itself remains largely a reactive system, however, emphasizing acute in-patient care over preventive care. ObamaCare [Patient Protection and Affordable Care Act, passed in 2010] includes money for some promising projects that focus care on the small number of patients—including many of the elderly—who drive the rise in health care spending. But Republicans are determined to wipe these out along with the rest of the law.

Raising Awareness of the Retirement Crisis

While the right and center-right beaver away at schemes to cut supports for seniors and their families, a few voices are trying to raise awareness of the retirement crisis.

The Commission to Modernize Social Security, a coalition that includes labor-funded groups as well as ethnic advocates like the National Council of La Raza and the National Asian Pacific Center on Aging, released a report last October calling on Congress to update Social Security to fit the profile of what will soon be a "majority-minority" U.S. population, much of it low-income. The commission's "Plan for a New Future" includes eliminating the cap on income subject to payroll tax and making the Social Security benefit formula less generous for high earners. With the savings, the commission proposes four ideas for benefits improvement:

- Updating Social Security's special minimum benefit to 12% of the poverty level, to help people who worked largely in low paying jobs;

- Reversing the Reagan-era cancellation of survivors' benefits for students through age 22;

- Increasing benefits for low-income widowed spouses; and

- Providing benefits for unpaid caregivers.

In the Senate, Vermont's Bernie Sanders is promoting an amendment to the Older Americans Act that would increase funding for programs that directly benefit the elderly, including meals programs, senior centers, and services to help them find employment. Significantly, Sanders's bill would change the stated objective of the original, 1965 legislation from providing the elderly with "an adequate income in retirement in accordance with the American standard of living" to "economic security in later life in accordance with . . . ." Another Senate bill, introduced by Democrats Sherrod Brown of Ohio and Barbara Mikulski of Maryland, would change the formula used to calculate Social Security benefits to better reflect expenses the elderly face.

Investing in Our Aging Population

What makes all these proposals—incremental as they may be—so starkly different is that they accept the reality that the U.S., like other industrialized economies, is aging. No magic-bullet solution, like converting Social Security into personal investment accounts, is going to allow society to avoid addressing this change collectively—unless the elites prefer to let a much larger percentage of elderly working people sink into poverty. Instead, society will have to figure out collectively how best to adjust its policies on housing, health care, and many other vital needs to the fact of an aging population. Arguably, more money can be saved by finding better ways to prevent and treat Alzheimer's than by shoehorning seniors and their families into a consumer-empowered system of health care buying.

But that would require investing in old age—for instance, by increasing funding for research at the National Institute on Aging. The preference in Washington is simply to cut spending on the aged and transfer the cost to families and city- and county-level poor relief programs—just where it was lodged 77 years ago, before Social Security existed. The four ideas that the Commission to Modernize Social Security advanced have all been circulating for years; several were in Al Gore's 2000 presidential platform. None has ever enjoyed serious consideration on Capitol Hill.

Yet, the need for Social Security and other social protections keeps growing. In 1980, according to the Census Bureau, 30% of American households received Social Security, subsidized housing, unemployment insurance, or other government benefits. In third-quarter 2008, the figure was 44%. In 2010, a record 18.3% of total personal income in the U.S. consisted of payments from these programs—up from a fairly stable 12.5% from 1980 to 2000. The title of an article in the *Wall Street Journal* covering this trend indicates the attitude of most members of the policymaking elite: "Obstacle to Deficit Cutting: A Nation on Entitlements." But one reason the public remain loyal to Social Security is their quite realistic assessment that they can't get its modest but essential benefits anywhere else.

It would cost a 66-year-old male $128,000 to purchase an annuity providing $10,000 a year for life, according to one estimate; a woman the same age would have to pay some $138,000. An annuity paying out $40,000 a year—a more realistic income requirement for most people—would cost about $550,000. A survey by the Employee Benefit Research Institute found that less than half of workers had $25,000 in savings, while only one-third had saved $50,000 or more. Most life insurance companies don't offer inflation-protected annuities—essential for retirees expecting to live a long time—and those that do, charge more.

What would happen if a proposal similar to Bowles-Simpson—the gold standard of the center-right—was enacted? Contrary to its sponsors' assertions, older workers would be affected very quickly by the stingier benefits formula. But most of the impact would be felt by workers who retire beginning in the 2020s. Gradually eroding benefits would force retirees to rely more on SSI and disability insurance and other forms of relief from state and local governments. Costs would go up for those governments. They, in turn, would move to cut costs. End result: a growing burden on retirees, their families and communities, and on non-profit relief organizations.

Media Coverage of the Crisis

The media don't ignore, exactly, the plight of the elderly, the ways in which the system of public support that did so much to lift them out of poverty in the pre-Reagan decades is now failing them, and the refusal of Washington and the private sector to prepare for their needs in coming years. Articles and features appear fairly often in major publications and on TV, radio, and the Internet.

But the corporate media almost never link the mounting problems facing the aged to the ongoing effort to slash Social Security, Medicare, and Medicaid. Even coverage of the 2011 and 2012 Republican House budget resolutions focused almost entirely on how deeply they would cut spending and the deficit, largely ignoring their impact on seniors and other at-risk groups. Since the major media tend to reflect the thinking of center-right Washington, this isn't unexpected.

This obliviousness explains why one of the fundamental concepts behind Social Security seldom makes it into the public discourse, and when it does, only to be dismissed. When mutual aid was translated into State-administered social insurance programs in Europe and—during the New Deal—in the U.S., it passed on the understanding that each generation owes a debt to the ones that came before—a debt it pays through, among other things, old-age pensions.

In place of this idea, Social Security's critics are attempting to implant the notion that each generation should begin and end with a clean balance sheet—that virtually any intergenerational "debt" is somehow unfair. This is an impossibility—or at least, a utopian vision that has never existed on earth. To journalists whose public-policy school is Capitol Hill and the think tank community, however, it sounds at least plausible—and more hard-headed than the idea of mutual aid. That's why pundits like the *New York Times'* David Brooks can reflexively describe "entitlements" as "fundamentally diseased" and dismiss politicians who balk at cutting them as "too ideologically rigid."

The tragedy of the three-decade debate over Social Security's future solvency isn't just that it's frozen the program in place, rendering any effort to update and improve benefits nearly impossible, but that it's desensitized the business and policymaking elite as well as the punditocracy to the needs of the very people Social Security was created to serve. Washington, both knowingly and unknowingly, is running away from the real retirement crisis, preferring to focus on a fiscal future that may be an illusion.

> *"The longer our nation delays making changes to the benefit and tax structures associated with entitlement programs for older individuals, the larger will be the 'legacy liability' that will be passed to future generations."*

An Aging Population Requires Reforms to Health Care and Social Security Programs

Committee on the Long-Run Macroeconomic Effects of the Aging U.S. Population, National Research Council

The Committee on the Long-Run Macroeconomic Effects of the Aging U.S. Population was appointed by the National Research Council to analyze a large body of academic research and provide a factual foundation for the social and political debates about population aging and policies regarding public entitlements. In the following viewpoint, the analysts report that the rising demographic shift in the United States will pose serious economic challenges and should be addressed with sensible policies. It is vital that the national response to the nation's changing demographics involve major structural changes to Social Se-

Excerpts from the *Report in Brief, Aging and the Macroeconomy: Long-Term Implications of an Older Population*, 2012. Reprinted with permission from Report Brief, 2012, by the National Academy of Sciences, Courtesy of the National Academies Press, Washington, D.C.

curity, Medicare, and Medicaid, they conclude. Other approaches should include encouraging workers to save more for retirement; raising taxes to pay for benefits; raising the retirement age; and reducing benefits. The authors believe that these changes need to be made now in order to smooth the transition to more effective and sustainable policies.

As you read, consider the following questions:

1. According to the authors, what is the US life expectancy projected to reach by 2050?

2. What does the Committee on Population cite as the US fertility rate from 2006–2010?

3. What percentage of the US workforce has an employer-sponsored retirement plan, according to the report?

The population of the United States will age substantially over the next four decades due to steadily rising longevity and the drop in fertility following the Baby Boom. Although longer life is a highly desirable improvement in human well-being, it also places stresses on our economic system because older people consume a great deal more than they earn through their market labor. To the extent that people have prepared for this stage of life by starting to save and accumulate assets earlier in their working lives, the problem is reduced, but in fact older people are substantially supported by public transfer programs such as Social Security, Medicare, and Medicaid.

Therefore, our national response will need to involve some combination of major structural changes to Social Security, Medicare, and Medicaid; higher savings rates during working years; and longer working lives. The longer our nation delays making changes to the benefit and tax structures associated with entitlement programs for older individuals, the larger will be the "legacy liability" that will be passed to future generations. The larger this liability, the larger the increase in taxes on future generations of workers, or the reduction in benefits for future generations of retirees, that will be required to restore fiscal balance. Decisions must be made now on how to craft a balanced response.

Fundamental Factors Shaping the Economic Landscape in the Coming Decades

As mortality rates have fallen in the U.S., the average length of life has risen from 47 years in 1900 to 78 today, and it is expected to continue to rise in coming decades. By 2050, U.S. life expectancy is projected to reach 84.5 years. The average person living now is much more likely to survive until age 65 or 70, and to live more years thereafter. This is aging at the level of the individual. Longer life is to be celebrated, and the discussion of the fiscal challenges that result should not distract from this key point. In addition, everyone who will reach age 65 by 2050 has already been born, as have many of the younger people who will be in the workforce then.

Health at older ages has also improved over the last half century as disability rates have fallen, and many of the additional years that people are living are healthy ones. However, the decline in disability appears to have stopped around 2000, and the future trend is uncertain. Nonetheless, the report found that there is substantial potential for increased labor force participation at older ages if people so choose. Most people will have plenty of healthy years still available at the time they retire. Later retirement is both a realistic policy option and an available individual choice.

In many countries including the United States, the age of 65 has conventionally been considered the "normal retirement age," and this chronological age has been incorporated into many public policies and private attitudes. The Committee believes that age 65 is an increasingly obsolete threshold for defining old age and for conditioning benefits for the elderly.

Shifting Balance of Older and Younger Population Groups

Longer life is only a part of the story. In 1957, at the height of the post-World War II Baby Boom, the fertility rate was 3.7 births per woman; the average for 2006–2010 was slightly less than 2.1 births per woman. Lower fertility causes slower population growth, and this is also a major cause of population aging. It makes younger age groups smaller relative to older ones, so there are fewer young people to support older people through taxes or private transfers.

The shifting balance of older and younger population groups has given rise to an increasingly contentious debate within American society about how to address fiscal deficits. Projected costs of public entitlement programs seem daunting, particularly in the context of economic recession. The historically large deficits of the last three years, in part caused by efforts to help the economy recover from the deep recession that followed the financial crisis in 2008, have unfortunately coincided with the leading edge of the retirement of the Baby Boom generation.

The Impacts of a Changing Global Economy

Whatever the economic consequences of population aging for the United States, it is important to recognize that the U.S. economy is integrated in the global economy and that population aging is a global, not merely a national, phenomenon. For example, level of income is a factor in international markets as well. Per capita income depends on both the fraction of the population employed and the average productivity per person employed. One of the ingredients in productivity growth comes, over the long run, from the generation and diffusion of new scientific, technological, and engineering knowledge as well as other gains in efficiency. While having a

What Is Demography?

Demography is the study of the growth, change, and structure of the human population. Changes in a population's size and structure are caused by changes in the birthrate, the death rate, and the net migration rates. Demographic research focuses on why people have the number of children they do; on factors that affect death rates; and on the reasons for immigration, emigration, and geographic mobility. Understanding a society's demography is an essential tool in determining current and future public health needs.

Anne R. Pebley, Encyclopedia of Public Health, *vol. 2, 2002.*

young population can help drive invention and innovation, population aging has very little effect on technological change across societies.

Other global factors, such as income levels, education, institutions, and economic incentives to innovate, tend to dominate the actual distribution of scientific and technological output. In addition, several factors may offset or amplify the decline in the number of workers per capita and increasing consumption pressures. These could include changes in underlying productivity growth, in labor force behavior, and in government policies, such as those influencing the growth in public and private health care costs.

In the United States, the weak economy that has followed the global financial crisis has ended many working careers prematurely. Meanwhile it also has lowered the value of many other components of household net worth, such as corporate equities and housing stock value, leaving many people ill-prepared to support themselves in retirement. Employment has grown faster than population over recent decades, but this trend is likely to reverse and there will be a slower growth in average incomes due to demographic trends. However, there might be other offsetting factors, either positive or negative, that would change the growth in living standards.

Four Practical Approaches to Prepare for Population Aging

Some combination of the following four approaches must be taken in order to prepare the United States for its future demographic distribution.

Workers save more (and consume less) in order to prepare better for their retirements.

Studies of the adequacy of U.S. retirement savings produce different answers depending upon the methods used, with research suggesting that between one-fifth and two-thirds of the older population have under-saved for retirement. Some common themes emerge. First, there is strong evidence that low- and lower-middle-income households accumulate few financial and pension assets for retirement. For these households, Social Security, Medicare, and Medicaid are a central part of maintaining living standards in retirement. To the extent that benefits paid by these government programs might be reduced in the future, the living standards of affected retiree households will fall.

Second, the quality of people's financial decisions, and therefore their financial literacy, will play an increasingly important role in how well households fare in their retirement years. Households will need to decide how much more to save and how to structure their portfolios during their working years. They will need to decide when it is economically prudent to retire, taking into account personal, macroeconomic, and political uncertainties. When they do retire, they will need to decide whether to annuitize their accumulations, and if so, how much and with what annuity options. For many households whose wealth rests mainly in their home ownership, they will need to decide whether and how to use those assets to finance consumption in retirement. There is substantial value in boosting financial literacy to help people prepare for these financial decisions.

Workers pay higher taxes (and thus consume less) in order to finance benefits for older people.

Longer and healthier lives are a great benefit, not in themselves a cost. But it does not follow that these added years of healthy life can all be taken as post-retirement leisure, rather than having some devoted to working longer, postponing retirement or working longer hours before retirement. If all of the added years are taken as leisure, then consumption at all ages must be considerably reduced to pay for these new years of leisure through higher savings or higher taxes.

Because the government plays a particularly important role in financing consumption and healthcare for the elderly, many of the consequences of population aging will be focused on specific government programs rather than spread across the economy. For these programs, population aging will have a major effect on costs. Population aging already has led to projected shortfalls in the finances of Social Security, Medicare and Medicaid, and is likely to lead to increasing government budget deficits in the future.

The consequences for Social Security are predictable, and they can be addressed relatively easily by changing benefit formulas and increasing contributions. Programs providing health care and long term care, notably Medicare and Medicaid, are a different matter. Health care costs per eligible person have been growing substantially faster than per capita income for decades, and if this pattern continues, it will interact with population aging to drive up public health care expenditures substantially.

Benefits (and thus consumption) for older people are reduced so as to bring them in line with current tax and saving rates.

About half of the U.S. workforce is covered by an employer-sponsored retirement plan, and this has been true for the last half-century. But the structure of pension plans has changed dramatically over time. In the 1970s, most employer-sponsored pension plans were of the defined benefit (DB) variety, where payouts were based on an employee's earnings history, length of service, and retirement age.

Today, employer plans in the corporate sector have mostly converted to defined contribution (DC) pensions—for example, 401(k) or 403(b) plans. Participants must generally decide how much to contribute (sometimes with an employer match) and where to invest the funds, thus bearing capital market risk more directly. The changing nature of pensions has several implications. For example, with benefit amounts less closely tied to workers' earnings histories—particularly when employees have an option to contribute little or nothing to the accounts—individuals may have difficulty determining whether their saving is adequate for their retirement needs.

People work longer and retire later, raising their earnings and national output.

Age at retirement is central to population aging and its economic consequences. Raising the average age of retirement is one key alternative to reducing the consumption associated with leisure and enhancing people's ability to stretch their assets over their lifetimes. The average retirement age for men declined substantially in the U.S. throughout most of the 20th century. Although this trend stopped in the early 1990s and then reversed, men still retire at a much younger age than in the past, despite their better health and much longer lives. Women's average age at retirement has moved parallel to men's over recent decades, but it stabilized and began to rise somewhat later.

The report suggests that there will be a continued rise in the labor force participation rate of older Americans. Some have expressed concern that if older members of the population work longer, they will "take jobs away" from the young. Yet this has not happened in the past, nor has it occurred in other nations. In normal times, outside of deep business cycle recessions, the overall number of jobs is determined primarily by the size of the labor force. If anything, an increase in older workers is predicted to slightly increase the wage rates of young workers.

Addressing the Challenges

The bottom line is that the nation has many good options for responding to population aging. On the whole, America is strong and healthy enough to pay for increased years of consumption through increased years of work, if we so choose. Alternatively, we will be healthy enough to enjoy additional active years of retirement leisure if that is our decision, individually or collectively—this is provided we choose to reduce our consumption and start saving more for retirement earlier in our lives.

Nonetheless, there is little doubt that there will need to be major changes in the structure of federal programs. The transition to sustainable policies will be smoother and less costly if steps are taken sooner rather than later. An aging society need not have lower living standards, lower growth in innovation and productivity, or inefficiently high tax rates. But delaying decisions on how to adapt to our aging demographic structure will make the transition more difficult and costly. Many adjustments will have to be made, and no single feasible policy change is likely to be either an acceptable or a sufficient response to the dynamic challenge and opportunity of population aging. While many aspects of the future are uncertain, population aging is a certainty, and the long-term macroeconomic shifts must be addressed by the political process sooner rather than later.

> *"Along with Social Security, Medicare is an important reason why the American elderly, on average, do not suffer the poverty and social marginalization they did in the past."*

An Aging Population Is Bankrupting Medicare

Abdul El-Sayed

Abdul El-Sayed is a social epidemiologist and fellow at Demos, a nonpartisan public policy institute. In the following viewpoint, he investigates the reasons why Medicare is so expensive and in such serious financial trouble. El-Sayed finds that America's aging population has led to more Medicare beneficiaries, while higher life expectancies mean that people are living longer. Today, Medicare is insuring more Americans for longer periods of time than ever before, which is an unsustainable situation. In addition, declining fertility rates result in fewer people of working age paying into the program, further damaging its long-term financial viability. Despite this dire scenario, El-Sayed warns, it is essential to find a way to save the program because it has kept so many elderly Americans out of poverty.

As you read, consider the following questions:

1. How much did Medicare cost in total expenditures in 2010, according to El-Sayed?

2. How many beneficiaries of Medicare does the author cite there are in the United States?

3. According to the author, what is the average amount of time a person receives Medicare benefits?

Accounting for 12 percent of the federal budget, and costing $509 billion in total expenditures in 2010, Medicare is a massive expense. In [. . . this viewpoint], we set out four trends that are key to understanding the rising cost of Medicare.

The undeniably important trend we'll discuss here is actually a twofer, including both the massive growth of the elderly population between 1965 and present day, as well [as] the vast expanse in life expectancy in the intervening period.

In 1966, the year after Medicare was passed, there were an estimated 19 million beneficiaries. Today, that number looks more like 48 million. In fact, given the aging of the baby boomer generation in the coming decades, the number of Medicare beneficiaries, barring any changes to eligibility, is projected to jump to 81 million by 2030.

Life Expectancy

The past 45 years have also seen the life expectancy of the average American increase from about 70 years in 1965 to about 78 years today. In other words, the average American today can expect to live about eight years longer than his or her grandparents.

Now, when it was initially passed in 1965, it was only expected that Medicare would insure the average beneficiary for about 15 years, as that was the average life expectancy for someone who had already lived 65 years. And there were only 19 million beneficiaries.

What Is Medicare?

Medicare is the federal health insurance program for people who are 65 or older, certain younger people with disabilities, and people with end-stage renal disease (permanent kidney failure requiring dialysis or a transplant, sometimes called ESRD).

The different parts of Medicare help cover specific services:

Medicare Part A (Hospital Insurance). Part A covers inpatient hospital stays, care in a skilled nursing facility, hospice care, and some home health care.

Medicare Part B (Medical Insurance). Part B covers certain doctors' services, outpatient care, medical supplies, and preventive services.

Medicare Part C (Medicare Advantage Plans). A Medicare Advantage Plan is a type of Medicare health plan offered by a private company that contracts with Medicare to provide you with all your Part A and Part B benefits. . . .

Medicare Part D (Prescription Drug Coverage). Part D adds prescription drug coverage to Original Medicare, some Medicare Cost Plans, some Medicare Private-Fee-for-Service Plans, and Medicare Medical Savings Account Plans. These plans are offered by insurance companies and other private companies approved by Medicare. Medicare Advantage Plans may also offer prescription drug coverage that follows the same rules as Medicare Prescription Drug Plans.

"What Is Medicare?" Medicare.gov, 2012.

This sets up some pretty simple math, which we can use to compare the number of people over the number of years the policy was initially intended to cover them in 1965 as compared to today. If the average beneficiary was covered for 15 years, and there were 19 million beneficiaries, then Medicare was on the hook for about 285 million person-years of overall coverage in 1966.

Let's compare that to today's scenario. There are 48 million beneficiaries who are covered for an average of 19 years (average life expectancy for adults aged 65 years in 2009), meaning that Medicare is now responsible for about 912 million person-years of coverage, more than three times as much coverage as when Medicare was first passed in the mid-1960s.

So, assuming no changes in the cost of healthcare, demographic changes in the American population alone would account for a three-fold increase in the cost of Medicare.

US Fertility Rates

But there's another wrinkle to this story. Baby boomers didn't have nearly as many children as their parents did and the fertility rate continues to fall. Therefore, not only are there more elderly to care for today, but because of the shrinking number of working Americans per beneficiary as a result of lagging fertility, the number of workers paying into the pot per beneficiary is well below what it was in 1965 when Medicare was first passed. In 1965, for example, the ratio of American workers paying taxes to the number of Medicare beneficiaries was about 4.6 to every one. That's fallen to about 3.4 in 2010, and is projected to fall as low as 2.3 by 2030.

While it's impossible to decrease the growth in the number of elderly, it *is* possible to decrease the number eligible for Medicare benefits. In that regard, assuming the program was only intended to support the elderly through the last 15 years of their lives, on average, it might seem justifiable to increase the Medicare-eligible age to 69 years, for example, instead of 65. To support that argument, pundits and policymakers point to data that suggest that today's elderly are substantially wealthier than they were in the past.

In all, this seems like a fair policy at face value. But on closer inspection, the underlying logic is just a tad flawed. It's clear that along with Social Security, Medicare is an important reason why the American elderly, on average, do not suffer the poverty and social marginalization they did in the past. But that was the point of the policy in the first place, right? It's like a doctor who's recently prescribed a new blood pressure pill that has successfully lowered his patient's blood pressure arguing that because her pressure is now low, she should no longer use the pill.

To be sure, something *does* need to be done—but there are more effective and efficient ways of addressing the cost albatross.

| "An older America . . . need not be an
obituary for Medicare."

An Aging Population
Will Save Medicare

Michael Hodin

*Michael Hodin is the executive director of the Global Coalition
on Aging. In the following viewpoint, he suggests that America's
aging population is going to save Medicare by remaining economically and socially productive well past retirement age. Hodin argues that today's seniors have been rejecting societal stereotypes of the elderly, remaining vital in the workplace, the arts,
and popular culture. This is essential in light of the aging demographics in the nation. America must see its aging population as
an opportunity and formulate policies that help keep older
Americans productive, healthy, and happy in their later years, he
maintains.*

As you read, consider the following questions:

1. According to Hodin, how many baby boomers in the
   Unites States are there?

2. What percentage of Americans were eligible for Medicare in 1965, according to Hodin?

3. What percentage of Americans does Hodin estimate will be eligible for Medicare by 2030?

You know you've arrived at a real inflection point when fashion, politics, and the urban intelligentsia collide. In New York, Carmen Dell'Orefice (81) adorns promotional banners and blogs during the run-up to the Fall Fashion shows. At the 92nd Street Y on Manhattan's Upper East Side, Mayor [Ed] Koch (87) and former Fed[eral Reserve] Chairman Paul Volker (84) lead a talk to "share relevant information and wisdom" for NYC's unofficial intelligentsia. And in The Villages, Florida—the self-proclaimed "friendliest retirement hometown"—a newly-minted [vice-presidential candidate] Paul Ryan enters stage right with his vibrant mother (78) to declare how he and [presidential candidate] Governor [Mitt] Romney plan to "save Medicare."

This unlikely collision of Fashion Week, the fashionable Manhattan Y, and the impossibly unfashionable "retirement communities" of the Sunshine State speak of a larger cultural shift that is upon us. In this young century, we are witnessing a new old. We are witnessing the emergence of a new aging process where people remain healthy, active, and productive—not to mention beautiful, smart, and politically savvy—into their 60s, 70s, and 80s.

So it's no wonder that this new kind of aging—and its impact on Medicare—has become a watershed issue of the 2012 Presidential campaign. But for all the speeches delivered by the politicians and all the ink spilled by the cognoscenti, everyone is missing the point. It's not that the 77 million Baby Boomers in the U.S. are going to bankrupt Medicare. The point is just the opposite. However ironic it may seem, this new, gigantic aging cohort is going to save the social insurance program.

How, indeed, can the explosive demand brought by the unprecedented aging of the American population save a program that pays out to the aging?

Saving Medicare

Fully embraced, an active, productive aging is creating and will continue to create a culture shift in which "seniors" break out of traditional roles of "need" and "dependency" and become vibrant producers in our society. No longer the automatic recipients of government welfare—and popular pity and condescension—healthy, vital seniors will remain at the heart of social and economic life and spare the precious federal insurance dollars for those really in need. This is not FDR's [Franklin Delano Roosevelt] or LBJ's [Lyndon B Johnson] aging population, and we shouldn't treat it as such.

But this transformation of aging isn't just culturally liberating. It's also economically essential. In the United States, there will soon be more people over 65 than under 15. So we're not just witnessing a new kind of aging; we're seeing the emergence of a new kind of society, one where older adults outnumber children. From both a social and a financial point of view, how can we look these demographic realities in the eye and not re-think how we provide healthcare and other essential services to the aging?

When Medicare was created in 1965, only 10 percent of Americans were over 65 and eligible. Today, this number has crept to 13 percent, and by 2030 it will reach 20 percent. No matter your political bent, this arithmetic is irrevocable.

An older America, however, need not be an obituary for Medicare. In fact, if we embrace this progressive, optimistic view of aging, the purported Medicare crisis becomes an opportunity. It is no secret that the American economy is in rough shape right now, and something substantial needs to change in order to jumpstart growth. The cultural change that is going to save Medicare is the same changes that put the

U.S. economy back on track. If older adults remain at the heart of social and economic life, then the U.S.'s largest population segment will become the U.S.'s "demographic dividend."

Economists and demographers often refer to the "demographic dividend" as the working-aged population that is driving economic growth. For the past couple of decades, much of Asia, for example, is seen to have a demographic dividend because its 18-to-55 population is far larger than the over-55s. But this culture shift . . . overtaking fashion week and presidential politics reveals that the U.S.'s aging population is its demographic dividend.

Fundamentally, our current political dialogue has the Medicare issue completely backwards. It's not just that Medicare needs to change in order to survive in an era of an older society; it's that our idea of aging itself needs to change in order to allow Medicare to survive.

> "Elder financial exploitation is a complex, nationwide problem, and combating it effectively requires a concerted, ongoing effort on the part of states and localities, as well as support and leadership at the federal level."

There Needs to Be a National Strategy to Deal with the Financial Exploitation of the Aging

Kay E. Brown

Kay E. Brown is the director at the US Government Accountability Office (GAO). In the following viewpoint, she deems financial exploitation of the elderly an epidemic in the United States and calls for a national strategy to address the problem. Brown argues that because such exploitation can take many forms, it will require a determined effort from federal, state, and local agencies and will involve social services, criminal justice, and consumer protection systems. In many communities, there are encouraging initiatives and collaborative programs in place. However, Brown contends that there needs to be a cohesive and deliberate national strategy in order to effectively address the issue.

Kay E. Brown, "Elder Justice: Strengthening Efforts to Combat Elder Financial Exploitation," Testimony before the Senate Special Committee on Aging, US Government Accountability Office, November 15, 2012.

As you read, consider the following questions:

1. According to a recent study, as cited by the author, how much has financial exploitation cost older adults in America in 2010?

2. How many states have adopted the Uniform Power of Attorney Act, according to Brown?

3. What US government agency does Brown recommend to define and implement a national strategy to fight elder exploitation?

I am pleased to have this opportunity to present some of the results from the latest study in our body of work on elder justice issues. According to experts, the illegal or improper use of older adults' funds, property, or assets is reaching epidemic proportions in this country and has far-reaching effects on its victims and society in general. The money older adults lose in these cases is rarely recovered and this loss can undermine both the health of older adults and their ability to support and care for themselves. One study estimated that financial exploitation cost older adults at least $2.9 billion in 2010.

Older adults can be exploited by family members and friends, home care workers, legal guardians and other fiduciaries, as well as those in the financial services industry. They also often fall prey to mail, telephone, and internet scams that offer substantial lottery or other winnings in exchange for so-called taxes or fees. Because elder financial exploitation can take many forms, combating it involves state and local agencies, and their federal counterparts, across social services, criminal justice, and consumer protection systems.

Report Findings

My testimony today is based on our November 2012 report, which is being released to the public today. It describes the challenges states face in combating the many types of elder financial exploitation and the actions federal, as well as state and local agencies, are taking to overcome these challenges. To obtain this information we interviewed state and local officials from social services, criminal justice, and consumer protection agencies in California, Illinois, New York, and Pennsylvania— states that vary geographically, and have large elderly populations and a number of initiatives that aim to combat elder financial exploitation. We also identified and assessed the activities aimed at preventing or responding to elder financial exploitation of seven federal agencies; conducted in-depth reviews of six prosecuted elder financial exploitation cases that are a non-generalizable sample of elder financial exploitation cases; interviewed many experts in this subject area; and reviewed relevant documents and published research. We conducted this performance audit from November 2011 to November 2012 in accordance with generally accepted government auditing standards. Those standards require that we plan and perform the audit to obtain sufficient, appropriate evidence to provide a reasonable basis for our findings and conclusions based on our audit objectives. We believe that the evidence obtained provides a reasonable basis for our findings and conclusions based on our audit objectives. Our investigative activities were conducted in accordance with standards prescribed by the Council of the Inspectors General for Integrity and Efficiency.

Challenges to Eliminating Exploitation

We found that state and local social services, criminal justice, and consumer protection agencies face many challenges as they work to prevent and respond to elder financial exploitation. For example

- Officials in each of the four states we contacted cited the need for more safeguards to prevent exploitation by financial services providers, power of attorney agents, and paid in-home caregivers;

- Officials told us that older adults need more information about what constitutes elder financial exploitation and how to avoid it, but social services and law enforcement agencies do not always have the resources to promote public awareness in this area;

- Banks are well-positioned to recognize, report, and provide evidence supporting investigations in elder financial exploitation cases; however, many social services and law enforcement officials we spoke with indicated banks do not always recognize and report exploitation or provide the evidence needed to investigate it; and

- According to experts, collaboration between the social services system—which protects and supports victims— and the criminal justice system—which investigates and prosecutes crimes—can be an effective means of combating elder financial exploitation. However, officials in three of our four states noted that this collaboration can be difficult to achieve. These two systems do not respond to exploitation or carry out their work in the same way, so there can be difficulties communicating across disciplines and different views regarding limits on information sharing.

Formulating Solutions

In many of the locations we contacted, state or local agencies are actively pursuing solutions to at least some of these challenges and there are some federal initiatives as well that could help address them. When it comes to preventing the sale to older adults of unsuitable or fraudulent investments, the Securities and Exchange Commission (SEC) and the Bureau of Consumer Financial Protection (CFPB), have each taken steps to help older adults avoid being exploited. SEC and CFPB have conducted research related to investment fraud that targets older adults, and there is a link on SEC's website to Financial Industry Regulatory Authority (FINRA) information consumers can use to check a financial services provider's qualifications and to understand the many designations used by securities professionals. CFPB also plans to issue a report in early 2013 addressing how information about financial advisors and their credentials should be provided to older adults. To prevent exploitation by power of attorney agents and paid in-home caregivers, 13 states have adopted the Uniform Power of Attorney Act in its entirety, and Napa County, California, now requires paid in-home caregivers to submit to a background check and obtain a permit before they can be hired.

We found that law enforcement authorities in some locations have devoted resources to promoting public awareness of elder financial exploitation. For example, the Pennsylvania Attorney General's Office has published a guide on how seniors can avoid scams and fraud, and in Cook County, Illinois, the Senior Law Enforcement Academy within the Sheriff's Department instructs older adults in how to prevent elder financial exploitation. In addition, each of the federal agencies we reviewed independently produces educational materials that could help prevent elder financial exploitation.

Collaborative Efforts

We also identified state, local, and federal activities encouraging banks to work with social services and law enforcement, and activities to promote and support collaboration between the social services and criminal justice systems. Illinois, for example, requires bank employees to receive training in how to report exploitation. Although we could identify no federal requirements for banks to train employees to recognize or report elder financial exploitation, the Administration on Aging (AoA) is considering collaborating with one large national bank on a project to develop such training. Financial institutions are required to file Suspicious Activity Reports (SAR) of potentially illegal bank transactions that involve, individually

Three Types of Elder Financial Abuse Crimes

Crimes of occasion, or opportunity, are incidents of financial abuse or exploitation that occur because the victim is merely in the way of what the perpetrator wants. The elder has money, assets, and the like, and an occasion presents itself for the perpetrator to avail himself or herself of the resource. . . .

Conversely, crimes of desperation are typically those in which family members or friends become so desperate for money that they will do whatever it takes to get it. Many of these family members are dependent on the elder parent for housing and money. What exacerbates their desire for more money is often a heightened need for drugs, alcohol, their gender (i.e., men are frequently perpetrators of this in comparison to women), or some combination of the three. The exploiting family member or friend comes to believe that, in return for care (actual or perceived and however little that care may be), he or she is due compensation (money, possessions, etc.), and often on a continuing basis.

Finally, crimes of predation, or occupation, occur when trust is engendered specifically for the intention of financial abuse later. A relationship is built, either through a bond of trust created though developing a relationship (romantic or otherwise), or as a trusted professional advisor. The taking of assets is by stealth and cunning, by working his or her way into the trust and life of the elder only to take it all and leave the elder penniless and without a relationship that was important in his or her life.

MetLife Mature Market Institute, "The MetLife Study of Elder Financial Abuse: Crimes of Occasion, Desperation, and Predation Against America's Elders," June 2011.

or in the aggregate, at least $5,000 with the Financial Crimes Enforcement Network (FinCEN), which has issued an advisory to banks that describes elder financial exploitation and its indicators and asks banks to specify "elder financial exploitation" when applicable in their SARs.

In each of the four states we contacted, there are also local initiatives to help bridge the gap between social services and criminal justice agencies. In some Pennsylvania and New York counties, multidisciplinary groups meet to discuss and help resolve all types of elder abuse cases. The Philadelphia Financial Exploitation Task Force and financial abuse specialist teams in some California counties, on the other hand, concentrate only on elder financial exploitation cases. Some steps have also been taken at the federal level to promote and inform collaboration between the social services and criminal justice systems in states. For example, a few grants to combat elder abuse or other crimes from AoA and the Department of Justice have required or encouraged collaboration, such as the use of multi-disciplinary teams, in states.

A National Strategy

Elder financial exploitation is a complex, nationwide problem, and combating it effectively requires a concerted, ongoing effort on the part of states and localities, as well as support and leadership at the federal level. Each of the seven federal agencies we reviewed is working to address this problem in ways that are consistent with its mission. However, preventing and responding to elder financial exploitation also calls for a more cohesive and deliberate national strategy. The Elder Justice Coordinating Council (EJCC)—a group of federal agency heads charged with setting priorities, coordinating federal efforts, and recommending actions to ensure elder justice nationwide—can be the vehicle for defining and implementing such a national strategy. To this end, we are recommending that the EJCC develop a written national strategy for combating elder financial exploitation. We suggest that this strategy ensure coordination of public awareness activities across federal agencies; address the need to identify and disseminate promising practices and other information states and localities can use to prevent exploitation; educate the public; promote agency collaboration; and promote investigation and prosecution of elder financial exploitation. Our report also recommends a number of actions individual federal agencies should take to better support state and local social services and law enforcement agencies, such as studying the feasibility of requiring that consumer complaints to the Federal Trade Commission's (FTC) Consumer Sentinel Network database include victim's age or an indication of whether the complaint involves elder financial exploitation.

Periodical and Internet Sources Bibliography

The following articles have been selected to supplement the diverse views presented in this chapter.

Linda Bergthold	"Are Medicare and Social Security Safe Now?" *The Huffington Post*, January 22, 2013.
Richard Eskow	"Social Security and Medicare: Behind the Numbers and the Spin," *Crooks and Liars*, April 23, 2012.
Robert Field	"Is Medicare Going Bankrupt? Not Really," www.philly.com, May 20, 2011.
Elaina F. George	"The Decline and Fall of Medicare," *New Visions Commentary*, September 12, 2012.
Judith Graham	"How in the World Will We Care for All the Elderly?" *New York Times*, October 10, 2012.
Phillip Longman	"Think Again: Global Aging," *Foreign Policy*, November 2010.
Alice M. Rivlin	"The Great Medicare Compromise," The Brookings Institution, August 29, 2012.
Avik Roy	"Trustees: Medicare Will Go Broke in 2016, If You Exclude Obama's Double Counting," Forbes.com, April 23, 2012.
Geraldine Sealey	"US Elderly to Double in 25 Years," ABC News, February 6, 2013.
Natasha Singer	"The Financial Time Bomb of Longer Lives," *New York Times*, October 16, 2010.
Paul N. Van de Water	"Medicare Is Not 'Bankrupt': Health Reform Has Improved Program's Financing," Center on Budget and Policy Priorities, April 24, 2012.

Chapter 2

What Are the Social and Legal Issues Related to an Aging Population?

Chapter Preface

The global recession that began in late 2007 was devastating for older Americans. One of the major consequences of the economic downturn was a striking increase in the unemployment rate for older workers. According to the Bureau of Labor Statistics, at the beginning of the recession it was at 3.2 percent; by August 2010, it had climbed to a high of 7.3 percent. In July 2012, the unemployment rate for workers age 55 and older was 6.2 percent. The bureau also reported that once an older worker was unemployed, he or she stayed out of work significantly longer than younger counterparts. On the average, it took an older unemployed worker about a year to find a new job.

A number of employment experts regarded these statistics as not only the byproduct of a floundering US economy, but also evidence of age discrimination in the workplace. In addition, it seemed the younger generation was favored in society in general. The emphasis on youth in the workplace, in popular culture, and in the media had left older Americans feeling marginalized. According to a recent study by the AARP, 80 to 95 percent of Americans age 50 and older believe that "age bias is a fact of life."

Age discrimination in the workplace is not a new problem—and it has been particularly difficult to address. In the hiring and treatment of workers, age bias is regarded by many employment experts to be one of the last socially acceptable forms of discrimination in the United States. In 1967 the US Congress passed the Age Discrimination in Employment Act, a milestone piece of legislation in the fight against workplace discrimination. The act banned discrimination of workers 40 years of age and older in hiring, promotion, discharge, compensation, or terms of employment.

In his comments after signing the act on December 15, 1967, President Lyndon B. Johnson traced the need for the legislation to the high rate of unemployment for older American workers. "Those figures added up to a senseless and costly waste of human talents and energy," he wrote in his statement. "They showed that men and women who needed to work—who wanted to work—and who were able to work, were not being given a fair chance to work. The need for national action was clear."

In 2009, however, the US Supreme Court handed down a decision that limited the civil rights protections for older Americans. In *Gross v. FBL Financial*, the court heard the case of Jack Gross, an employee of FBL Financial, who was demoted from his job in 2003. Gross charged that the company demoted a group of a dozen older workers, including him, and transferred younger workers into their positions. Gross was the only one of the dozen to file an age discrimination lawsuit against his employer. The case went all the way to the Supreme Court, who held that a plaintiff in an age discrimination suit must prove, with a preponderance of evidence, that age was the reason for the discrimination. In effect, the Supreme Court decision made it much harder for older workers to protect themselves from age discrimination in the workplace.

"The Supreme Court's decision in my case significantly undermined well-established protections against discrimination for older workers," commented Jack Gross in a 2012 press release from Senator Tom Harkin. "I am also concerned that this decision, with my name on it, is being used as precedent to undermine workers' rights under other civil rights laws, too."

In recent years, lawmakers have proposed legislation to address the Supreme Court decision and extend protections to older American workers. Age discrimination is one of the subjects discussed in the following chapter, which touches on some of the social and legal issues pertaining to an aging population. Other viewpoints in the chapter examine media and popular culture stereotypes, the problem of aging drivers, and the need for strong legal protections for the elderly.

> *"Some employers don't see older workers as an asset to their organizations—and their negative views can prevent skilled, qualified people from contributing."*

Age Discrimination in the Workplace Is a Problem

Elizabeth Rogers

Elizabeth Rogers is a contributor to 50Plus.com, now a part of everythingzoomer.com, a lifestyle portal customized for the age 45-plus demographic. In the following viewpoint, she asserts that ageism in the workplace is still a major problem, with more and more age-related discrimination claims being filed every year. Rogers reports that the actual cases of age discrimination may be much higher. With more people working longer or returning to the workforce after retirement, it is necessary to emphasize the benefits of older workers and banish the damaging stereotypes that employers may have. There are a number of job-seeking strategies that can help people find jobs in a competitive job market and ways to combat harmful stereotypes about older workers.

As you read, consider the following questions:

1. According to the US Equal Employment Opportunity Commission, as cited by the author, how many age-related discrimination claims were filed under the Age Discrimination in Employment Act in 2011?

2. How many years of work experience should older workers include on their resume, according to Mary Eileen Williams and reported by the author?

3. As noted by Rogers, how does Williams say that an older job seeker should dress for a job interview?

Is a number keeping you from getting ahead, staying employed or finding that next opportunity? In 2009, we looked at how ageism affects people's careers. It's now 2012, and not much seems to have changed.

Remember the case of Arlene Phillips, then 66-year-old judge on a popular UK dancing show replaced by a host less than half her age? Three years later, the BBC still faces accusations of ageism. The *UK Telegraph* reports there are now up [to] 30 lawsuits involving ageism and sexism pending against the organization. One former presenter, Miriam O'Reilly, successfully sued the BBC and won a six-figure settlement.

Of course, it isn't just the entertainment industry that's affected. Stories like those of Adina Lebo and Barry Everatt aren't uncommon—both were let go from their jobs after decades of employment and faced challenges trying to find meaningful work.

And then there was the 2009 report about a rise in age-related discrimination claims filed with the U.S. Equal Employment Opportunity Commission (EEOC). Cases are still on the rise, according to the latest statistics. In 2009, 22,778 charges were filed under the Age Discrimination in Employment Act (which protects workers age 40 and over). In 2011, that number rose to 23,465.

© Mike Baldwin / Cornered

"I can't believe you'd accuse us of age discrimination. At your age, you ought to know better."

© Mike Baldwin / CartoonStock.com

Age Discrimination Is on the Rise

But take these numbers with a grain of salt. Experts warn they only represent the formal complaints workers have filed—the actual number of cases could be much higher. Many workers don't step forward because age discrimination is so difficult to prove, especially when it occurs during the hiring process. Of the cases filed with the EEOC, only about one sixth of cases end with a "merit resolution"—that is, an outcome that's favourable for the employee (like a cash settlement or a successful conciliation).

"Ageism in the workplace is still with us despite major gains over the years," says Susan Eng, Vice President of Advocacy at CARP. "CARP was successful in getting mandatory retirement prohibited at the federal level as it had done at the provincial level. But that only begins the process of eliminating discriminatory practices."

"Recognition that older workers bring a wealth of experience that could give an employer a competitive advantage and mentoring programs to allow older workers to share their knowledge would go a long way to countering the trend that older workers are losing their jobs for no other reason than that the employer has not taken the long view."

What else hasn't changed? Our population is still getting older. According to the latest census data, seniors (people age 65 and over) now make up a higher proportion of the population than ever before—and in a few years this group will be larger than the age 14 and under cohort. Over 42 per cent of our working age population (people ages 15 to 64) are between the ages of 45 and 64. About three in 10 people in Canada are members of the baby boomer generation.

Of course, the term "working age" is a bit of a misnomer. Survey after survey reports more people are working longer or are returning to the workforce after retirement. For some workers, it's a financial necessity, but for others it's a chance to stay engaged in a fulfilling career or try out a new opportunity.

Combating the Unspoken Stereotypes

Unfortunately, some employers don't see older workers as an asset to their organizations—and their negative views can prevent skilled, qualified people from contributing.

"They might not say it, but employers may be holding certain things against you," says Mary Eileen Williams, veteran career counselor and author of *Land the Job You Love: 10 Surefire Strategies for Jobseekers Over 50.*

For instance, Williams warns some employers might be thinking:

- You don't have the technical skills for the job. (Younger employees are often seen as being more tech-savvy than their older colleagues.)

- You won't want to report to a younger boss. (Some employers assume older workers have an age bias against younger workers too.)

- You're tired, slow and unenthusiastic. (Younger workers are often seen as being more energetic and innovative.)

- You're just marking time until you retire. (Why take the time and expense to train someone who doesn't plan on staying long?)

- You have health problems that will require you to take more time off. (Or be a drain on employer insurance policies.)

Unfair? You bet—especially when experts note that there's often more variation among workers in the same age group than there is between different groups.

Tips for Job Hunting

So what can you do if you're job hunting and worried your age might be a barrier? Here are some of Williams' top tips:

Craft your applications accordingly. Time to rethink that resume so it provides the right amount of information about you—without giving too much away about your age. Williams says most applicants need only include the last 15–20 years of work experience, and it's okay to list 20+ years working in a given field even if that number is a little higher.

You can also adapt the resume format to best suit your skills and experience. For example, a "hybrid" resume that combines elements of a functional resume and chronological resume can let you highlight your skills and accomplishments without risking information overload or leaving gaps. However, don't try to hide too much in the process.

"Don't create at resume that makes you look 28 if you're actually 58," warns Williams. "Otherwise employers will feel misled when they meet you."

Focus on networking. It's good advice for job seekers of any age, but even more important for mature workers, says Williams. The longer you've been in the workforce, the better developed your professional network is—and the more likely you are to have connections who know people in decision-making positions.

"That personal reference speaks to your talent and work ethic. It's like being pre-screened for an interview," Williams says. "The older you are, the more likely you are to get your job through networking."

Dress appropriately. Like it or not, how you look makes an impression. You don't have to hide your grey hair, but an up-to-date hair style and makeup shows you're current and "in touch". The same goes for your outfit and shoes—if they're well worn and dated, they'll make you seem worn out and dated too. Dressing appropriately for the position and your body type can help you appear youthful and energetic.

Convey confidence. What about those worries about your health, energy and enthusiasm? What you wear and what you say is just part of the equation, says Williams. You can also convey energy, enthusiasm and confidence with non-verbal cues like good posture, a firm handshake and facial expressions. Always look your interviewer in the eye, she says, and open up your body language.

Address unspoken concerns. Chance are an employer isn't going to directly ask how you feel about working with younger employees or reporting to a younger boss. Williams says mature job seekers can be proactive and bring up the topic in an interview. You can comment on the age-diverse workplace, for example, and say how you enjoy working with people of all ages and have learned a lot from younger colleagues. Likewise, if you have reported to a younger boss in the past, mention how it's never been a problem for you.

What about the misconception that you're killing time until retirement? Williams notes you can turn the tables by asking about opportunities for growth and training within the company.

Keep up with your technical skills—and show them off. Demonstrating a willingness to acquire new skills and keep current with technology can also help dispel some misconceptions about your age. Let interviewers know that technology is not a problem for you, and give examples of new skills and applications you've learned.

"If you don't have the right computer skills, get them," says Williams. "Try an online tutorial or a class."

And perhaps the most important piece of advice: don't make the mistake of thinking you're "less than" because of your age. Williams reminds to focus on the positive—all the experience and skills you can bring to a position. At every step of the application process, remind potential employers that your skills and experience are just what they're looking for.

It's a little easy to get lost in the rhetoric about ageism in the workplace, but knowing about the potential stereotypes shouldn't discourage you. Knowing about them means you can work to counteract them. As our population continues to age, you can bet age-related discrimination in the workforce isn't going to go away anytime soon.

"Older Americans are doing better than in the past and younger ones doing worse."

Age Discrimination in the Workplace Is Not a Problem

Diana Furchtgott-Roth

Diana Furchtgott-Roth is a senior fellow at the Manhattan Institute for Policy Research, a conservative think tank that emphasizes economic choice and individual responsibility. In the following viewpoint, she observes that recent studies show that although older workers are having a tough time finding employment in today's workplace, younger workers have higher rates of unemployment than older workers. In fact, older Americans hold a number of advantages over younger Americans: they have less debt, have higher incomes, and have benefited from appreciation of their homes. Instead of focusing on creating new programs to boost employment for older workers, policy makers should focus on eliminating burdensome regulations and supporting job creators.

Diana Furchtgott-Roth, excerpted from "Missed by the Recovery: Solving the Long-Term Unemployment Crisis for Older Workers," Testimony Before the Special Committee on Aging, United States Senate, One Hundred Twelfth Congress, Second Second Session, May 15, 2012.

As you read, consider the following questions:

1. According to a US Government Accountability Office report cited by the author, what was the unemployment rate for older works at the end of 2011?

2. According to US Census Bureau statistics presented by the author, how many Americans live in poverty?

3. According to a *Wall Street Journal* article mentioned by Furchtgott-Roth, what percentage of new jobs created by US multinationals were offshore?

Chairman Kohl, Ranking Member Corker, members of the Committee, I am honored to be invited to testify before you today on the employment situation of America's senior citizens. The employment problems that senior citizens face are indeed serious, and I thank you for holding this hearing.

I am a senior fellow at the Manhattan Institute. From 2003 until April 2005 I was chief economist at the U.S. Department of Labor. From 2001 until 2002 I served at the White House Council of Economic Advisers as chief of staff. I have served as Deputy Executive Secretary of the Domestic Policy Council under President George H.W. Bush and as an economist on the staff of President Reagan's Council of Economic Advisers.

The new U.S. Government Accountability Office report, entitled "Many Experience Challenges Regaining Employment and Face Reduced Retirement Security," provides sobering data on older workers. More than half of unemployed workers age 55 and over have been unemployed for 27 weeks or longer. The unemployment rate for these workers was 6.6 percent at the end of 2011.

It is especially important to address this problem due to the aging of the workforce and the entry of the Baby Boom generation into retirement. Older workers can expect to live until their mid-80s, sometimes longer, and dropping out of the labor force at 55 could mean 30 years of retirement. Such lengthy retirements mean that a larger older population is supported by a smaller younger population.

More urgently, our economy should be structured so that all those who want to work can find jobs. Millions of Americans are looking for work, and the number in poverty, 46.2 million, is the highest since the Census Bureau began compiling poverty data 52 years ago.

Younger workers are also finding a shortage of jobs. Page 9 of the GAO report shows that, as tough as older workers have it in today's labor market, their unemployment rates are lower than workers aged 25 to 64 and workers aged above 16. And, on page 18 of the report, the authors present evidence that since 2000 the labor force participation rates of workers 55 and over have been rising steadily, whereas the labor force participation rates of workers aged 16 to 24 and workers aged 25 to 54 have been declining. The biggest decline in labor force participation rates, according to GAO, can be observed for workers aged 16 to 24.

Despite the evidence that younger workers are worse off than older workers, the GAO report recommends that Congress offer temporary wage and training subsidies to employers who hire older workers who have experienced long-term unemployment; that Congress eliminate the requirement that Medicare is the secondary payer for workers covered by employer-provided health insurance; that Congress expand job search and training programs for older workers; and that Congress compensate older workers for accepting lower-paying, full-time jobs.

No cost estimate is provided for these programs, although the unnamed experts cited on pages 46 and 47 estimate that they "could be expensive" or "would cost money." Neither is any estimate of benefits provided, such as how much the duration of unemployment would be reduced if these programs were funded.

The GAO study lacks rigor in other ways too. It is filled with anecdotes from "focus groups" and "experts." Only 77 people were used in the focus groups, a remarkably small sample. The focus groups were interviewed in three cities, namely San Jose (California), Baltimore, and St. Louis. These cities are not representative of the United States as a whole.

Furthermore, the selection of the focus groups and experts is undocumented. Were employed seniors as well as unemployed seniors interviewed? The study purports to be a "performance audit" and that it meets "generally accepted government auditing standards," a rather vague term that certainly does not mean that the study was subjected to an outside independent review or audit. All of this effort took 18 months to prepare at taxpayer expense.

According to GAO, the main characteristic of older workers that makes them qualify for extra government help is the share unemployed for 27 weeks or longer. Fifty-five percent are out of work for 27 weeks or longer, compared to 47 percent for workers aged 25 to 54, and 35 percent for young adults ages 20 to 24. Other than that, they are better off than other groups.

What is striking is that over the past ten years employment has increased among Americans 55 and over by 8.9 million. At the same time, it has declined by 3.1 million in the 25 to 54 age group, and by 313,000 among those aged 20 to 24.

[The report] shows how the labor force participation rate of seniors has increased by 5.7 percentage points from 2002 to 2011, yet declined in other age groups.

Compared with those aged 20 to 24 and 25 to 54, unemployment rates are lowest for the 55+ age group and have seen the smallest increase. Older Americans have seen unemployment rates rise by 2.8 percentage points over the past 10 years. Unemployment rates have risen by 4.9 percentage points for the 20 to 24 age group, and by 3.1 percentage points for Americans aged 25 to 54.

During some periods labor force participation rates have risen for older women and declined for older men. This is not true over the past decade. Both men and women ages 55 and over have seen similar increases in labor force participation rates.

This pattern holds for men and women ages 65 and over. Both labor force participation rates and employment levels have risen steadily over the past 10 years.

The unemployment rate in 2011 for newly graduated men and women with bachelor's degrees was 9 percent, far higher than the 4.9 percent rate such young adults experienced in 2006. The effects of the recession have fallen most disproportionately on them. These unemployment rates not only suggest personal disappointment, but also large and lasting implications for them and for society. A recent paper in the *American Economic Journal: Applied Economics* found that graduating in a recession leads to earnings losses that last for 10 years after graduation.

The authors, University of Toronto economics professor Philip Oreopoulos, Columbia University professor Till von Wachter, and economist Andrew Heisz of Statistics Canada, found that earnings losses are greater for new entrants to the labor force than for existing workers, who might see smaller raises, but who have jobs. In addition, recessions lead workers to accept employment in small firms that pay lower salaries.

In addition to higher unemployment rates, large increases in college tuition in recent decades mean that young people are graduating with substantial debt. According to Howard Dvorkin, founder of Consolidated Credit Counseling in Fort Lauderdale, students who graduated in 2011 left school with almost $23,000 in student loans, the most ever.

That is one reason why rates of recent graduates living at home with either a parent or grandparent have increased. In 2005 the share of 20–24-year-olds who had at least a bachelor's degree but were living at home was 36 percent, and it reached 43 percent in 2011.

In November 2011 the Pew Research Center issued a lengthy study entitled "The Rising Age Gap in Economic Well-Being," which concluded that the gap in well-being between the young and the old is greater than ever before. Older Americans are doing better than in the past and younger ones doing worse. I attach the study, and I respectfully request that it is entered into the record.

Pew concludes that older Americans have benefited from appreciation of their homes, higher incomes, and lower unemployment rates. When these factors are taken into account, older Americans come out ahead of younger Americans. According to Pew, between 1984 and 2009, median net worth fell by 68 percent for households headed by adults younger than 35, and rose by 42 percent for households headed by those over 65. (Net worth is the value of assets less debt.)

The older age group had 47 times the net wealth of the younger group in 2009, compared to a multiple of 10 a quarter century earlier. It's not surprising that older people have more wealth, because they have been saving longer and building the equity in homes they own. That the ratio has risen so much is a result of contraction of net worth among the young and expansion for the seniors.

Older Americans who bought houses or condos have seen their home equity rise because they have held their homes for longer periods of time. The 2009 American Housing Survey reports that 50 percent of older Americans bought their homes before 1986, and 65 percent own their homes free of mortgages.

In contrast, younger Americans who own homes have seen them decline in value, particularly if they bought them during the housing boom of the previous decade.

As well as assets, Pew reports that incomes of older Americans have risen four times as fast as incomes of younger Americans. Compared to 1967, incomes of Americans 65 and older have risen by 109 percent, after adjusting for inflation, but incomes of adult Americans under 35 have risen by a far smaller amount, 27 percent. The inflation-adjusted median income of older Americans rose by 8 percent between 2005 and 2010, but the income of younger Americans declined by 4 percent.

As the GAO report states, the problem not just for senior citizens but for all Americans is too few jobs. The Labor Department issued another disappointing jobs report on May 4 [2012], showing that in April only 115,000 jobs were created in the economy, and the unemployment rate declined to 8.1 percent because another 342,000 people left the labor force. One reason that the employment picture is bleak is because it's getting harder to create jobs due to our regulatory environment.

Mr. [Barack] Obama acknowledged this when, on May 10, 2012, he issued an executive order expanding Executive Order 13563, which was entitled "Improving Regulation and Regulatory Review." The May 10 Executive Order asks for public input in reducing regulations, and calls on agencies to prioritize their regulatory reviews to deal with the most burdensome regulations first.

Tougher regulations lead employers to locate elsewhere. Friendlier regulations draw them back home.

One proposed bill that would interfere with job creation is S. 1471, the Fair Employment Opportunity Act of 2011. The bill would set up another protected class of workers, the unemployed. The unemployed would be allowed to sue employers for discrimination, just as women can sue for sex discrimination, older people can sue for age discrimination, and different minorities can sue for racial discrimination.

The bill, sponsored by Connecticut Senator Richard Blumenthal, has two cosponsors. It purports to solve the problem of the long-term unemployed finding jobs, but it would slow job creation and make it harder for everyone, including the long-term unemployed, to find jobs.

Christine Owens, executive director of the National Employment Law Project, has testified that "There is no official data on how frequently unemployed workers are denied consideration for jobs because of their employment status." This so-called problem is just based on anecdotal evidence. Monster.com, an online job search Web site, has stated that fewer than one hundredth of one percent of its job search ads excluded the unemployed.

Penalties that the courts could levy on employers and employment agencies would be heavy, including back-pay, $1,000 per violation per day, and punitive damages.

This would increase the cost of hiring American workers, making it more likely that employers will expand plants offshore. Employers would face more paperwork to show that they are not discriminating against the unemployed, and trial lawyers would target companies with threats of lawsuits.

Already, it is easier to employ workers overseas than in the United States, and the Fair Employment Opportunity Act of 2011 would add to that. *The Wall Street Journal* reported on April 27 that three-quarters of new jobs created by U.S. multinationals were offshore over the past two years.

Rather than pass yet another bill discouraging employers from creating jobs, how about some sensible solutions to generate jobs.

- Add more certainty to the tax system. Rates on income and capital are scheduled to rise dramatically next January 1, creating extensive uncertainty.

- Eliminate the Environmental Protection Agency's new regulations on coal, which are affecting the utility sector, which employs a disproportionate number of older workers. Over 100 coal-fired plants have closed since January 2010.

- Approve the Keystone XL Pipeline, so that Canadian oil could go to our refiners in the Gulf to be made into gasoline and other products.

- Remove the $2,000 worker per year penalty in the new health care law paid by employers with more than 49 full-time workers who don't offer the right kind of health insurance. Going from 49 to 50 workers will cost some employers $40,000 per year beginning in 2014.

- Extend and expand the EB-5 visa program for foreigners who want to start companies in America, so that innovators can come and create jobs. The program is due to expire in September 2012. Americans are facing an employment problem on a scale that our government at times seems incapable of grasping. We need to think of ways to turn America around and head all of us in the right direction by generating jobs here at home. That will help older American workers and younger ones at the same time.

Thank you for inviting me to appear here today. I would be glad to answer any questions.

> *"Although long-term unemployment hurts job seekers of all ages, it poses particular challenges for older workers."*

New Strategies Are Needed for Aging Job Seekers

Charles A. Jeszeck

Charles A. Jeszeck is a director at the US Government Account-ability Office (GAO). In the following viewpoint, Jeszeck testifies before a Senate committee about a recent GAO report on the problem of long-term unemployment and its effect on older American workers. Jeszeck reports that older workers tend to be out of work longer than younger workers, forcing many older workers to take money from their retirement savings. When older workers do find work, they may receive lower wages and find it difficult to replace their retirement savings. It is essential to identify new strategies to address the major reemployment challenges posed by older workers. Jeszeck recommends that policy makers from the Department of Labor would be appropri-ate for that task.

As you read, consider the following questions:

1. According to Jeszeck, what was the unemployment rate for older workers in April 2012?

Charles A. Jeszeck, "Unemployed Older Workers: Many Face Long-Term Joblessness and Reduced Retirement Security," Testimony Before the Special Committee on Aging, US Senate, May 15, 2012.

2. What percentage of all unemployed older workers does Jeszeck testify had been unemployed for over a year by 2011?

3. What did many experts cite, according to the author, as the key reason employers are reluctant to hire older workers?

I am pleased to be here today to discuss the status of unemployed older workers. The most recent recession, which began in 2007 and ended in 2009, was the worst since the Great Depression and has been characterized by historically high levels of long-term unemployment. While it is crucial that the nation help people of all ages return to work, long-term unemployment has particularly serious implications for older workers (age 55 and over). Job loss for older workers threatens not only their immediate financial security, but also their ability to support themselves during retirement.

My remarks today summarize a report that we prepared for this committee and released today. My testimony will focus on (1) how the employment status of older workers age 55 and over has changed since the recession, (2) older workers' challenges in finding new jobs, (3) how periods of long-term unemployment might affect older workers' retirement income, and (4) what other policies might help unemployed older workers regain employment and what steps the Department of Labor (Labor) has taken to help unemployed older workers.

To examine changes in the employment status of older workers since the start of the recession, we analyzed nationally representative unemployment and demographic data from the Bureau of Labor Statistics (BLS), including January 2007 through April 2012 data from the Current Population Survey (CPS) and the 2008 and 2010 Displaced Worker Supplement (DWS). To learn about older workers' challenges in finding new jobs, we conducted focus groups with unemployed older workers in four metropolitan areas and interviewed staff at one-stop career centers in each of the four areas. Further, we interviewed experts on older workers' issues and reviewed studies. To assess how periods of long-term unemployment might affect older workers' retirement income, we used micro-simulation models, and interviewed officials at the Social Security Administration (SSA). To identify what policies might help unemployed older workers regain employment and what Labor has done to help older workers, we interviewed experts on policy proposals previously identified through a review of the literature and interviewed Labor officials.

We conducted this performance audit from October 2010 through April 2012 in accordance with generally accepted government auditing standards. Those standards require that we plan and perform the audit to obtain sufficient, appropriate evidence to provide a reasonable basis for our findings and conclusions based on our audit objectives. We believe that the evidence we obtained provides a reasonable basis for our findings and conclusions based on our audit objectives.

Background on Social Security and Employer-Sponsored Retirement Plans

Social Security retirement benefits are paid to eligible workers under the Old-Age, Survivors, and Disability Insurance (OASDI) program administered by SSA. The level of monthly retirement benefits an individual will receive depends on factors such as work and earnings history and the age at which the beneficiary chooses to begin receiving benefits. Generally, individuals may begin receiving Social Security retirement benefits at age 62; however, the payments will be lower than if they wait to receive benefits at their full retirement age, which varies from 65 to 67, depending on the individual's birth year. Social Security also provides benefits to eligible workers who become disabled before reaching retirement age, as well as children, spouses, and widow(er)s of eligible workers.

Employer-sponsored retirement plans fall into two broad categories: defined benefit (DB) plans and defined contribution (DC) plans. DB plans promise to provide a benefit that is determined by a formula based on particular factors specified by the plan, such as salary or years of service. Typically, DB plans provide annuity payments to retirees on a monthly basis that continue as long as the recipient lives. Under DC plans, workers and employers may make contributions into individual accounts. At retirement, participants' distribution options vary depending on the plan, but often include leaving their money in the plan or taking a full or partial distribution. In order to preserve the tax benefits from their DC plan savings, many participants choose to roll plan savings into an individual retirement account (IRA). IRAs are personal retirement savings arrangements that allow individuals to make contributions to an individual account and receive favorable tax treatment.

Long-Term Unemployment for Older Workers Has Increased Substantially

Unemployment rates for workers of all ages have risen dramatically since the start of the recent recession in December 2007, and workers age 55 and over have faced particularly long periods of unemployment. [The] seasonally unadjusted unemployment rate for older workers increased from 3.1 percent in December 2007 to a high of 7.6 percent in February 2010, before it decreased to 6.0 percent in April 2012. As in prior recessions, smaller percentages of workers age 55 and over became unemployed in comparison with younger workers. Some researchers attribute older workers' lower unemployment rates to the fact that older workers tend to have longer job tenure, and are consequently less likely to be laid off than younger workers.

Although older workers are less likely than younger workers to lose their jobs, it generally takes older job seekers longer to find new work. Since 2007, many job seekers of all ages have experienced long-term unemployment, but individuals age 55 and over have consistently experienced longer durations of unemployment than younger workers. Moreover, the median length of unemployment has more than tripled for older workers since the recession started, increasing at a greater rate than that of younger workers. Prior to the recession, the median duration of unemployment for job seekers age 55 and over was 10 weeks compared with 9 weeks for job seekers aged 25–54. By 2011, the median duration of unemployment for older job seekers had increased to 35 weeks compared with 26 weeks for younger job seekers. In 2007, less than a quarter of unemployed older workers were unemployed for longer than 27 weeks. . . . By 2011, this number had increased to 55 percent. Moreover, by 2011 over one-third of all unemployed older workers had been unemployed for over a year.

Rates of unemployment for older workers varied across demographic groups. Unemployment rates for older men were comparable to those of women in 2007 but were significantly higher for men by 2011. In addition, black and Hispanic older workers had significantly higher unemployment rates than white older workers in both 2007 and 2011. Regarding education level, older workers without a high school diploma were more likely to be unemployed before and after the recession than those with a high school diploma. However, the unemployment rate for workers with at least a bachelor's degree approximately doubled by 2011 from its 2007 level, just as it did for those older workers with less education.

Across several different demographic groups, once unemployed, older workers were similarly likely to remain unemployed for more than half a year (27 weeks or more) in 2011. For example, in 2011 older unemployed workers with at least a bachelor's degree were similarly likely to face long-term unemployment as those older workers with less education. In addition, older workers in each racial or ethnic group who became unemployed were equally likely to face long-term unemployment in 2011. Even older women—who in 2007 had lower rates of long-term unemployment than men—were similarly likely to face long-term unemployment after the recession.

We analyzed the earnings of workers who regained employment after being displaced from their jobs from 2007 to 2009 and found that older workers generally sustained greater earnings losses than younger workers. When comparing earnings before and after displacement, the median earnings replacement rate for workers aged 55–64 who were displaced from 2007 to 2009 was only 85 percent, compared with approximately 95 percent for workers aged 25–54 and over 100 percent for workers aged 20–24. Further, an estimated 70 percent of reemployed displaced older workers sustained earnings losses (an earnings replacement rate of less than 100 percent) compared with 53 percent of reemployed individuals aged 25–54.

Reluctance to Hire Older Workers Is Perceived as a Challenge

Focus group participants told us that they believed employer reluctance to hire older workers was their primary reemployment challenge, and several cited job interview experiences that convinced them that age discrimination was limiting their ability to find a new job. Moreover, many experts, one-stop career center staff, and other workforce professionals we interviewed said that some employers are reluctant to hire older workers. Because of legal prohibitions against age discrimination, employers are unlikely to explicitly express a lack of interest in hiring older workers; however, one workforce professional told us that local employers had asked her to screen out all applicants over the age of 40.

According to experts we interviewed, a key reason employers are reluctant to hire older workers is that employers expect providing health benefits to older workers would be costly.

What Is Age Discrimination?

Age discrimination involves treating someone (an applicant or employee) less favorably because of his age.

The Age Discrimination in Employment Act (ADEA) only forbids age discrimination against people who are age 40 or older. It does not protect workers under the age of 40, although some states do have laws that protect younger workers from age discrimination.

It is not illegal for an employer or other covered entity to favor an older worker over a younger one, even if both workers are age 40 or older.

Discrimination can occur when the victim and the person who inflicted the discrimination are both over 40.

Age Discrimination and Work Situations. The law forbids discrimination when it comes to any aspect of employment, including hiring, firing, pay, job assignments, promotions, layoff, training, fringe benefits, and any other term or condition of employment.

Age Discrimination and Harassment. It is unlawful to harass a person because of his or her age. Harassment can include, for example, offensive remarks about a person's age. Although the law doesn't prohibit simple teasing, offhand comments, or isolated incidents that aren't very serious, harassment is illegal when it is so frequent or severe that it creates a hostile or offensive work environment or when it results in an adverse employment decision (such as the victim being fired or demoted).

"Age Discrimination,"
US Equal Employment Opportunity Commission, *2012.*
www.eeoc.gov.

Several surveys of employers corroborate this concern. A few focus group participants we spoke to who had handled their previous employer's health insurance or had been involved in hiring decisions said they had seen that older workers substantially increased insurance costs, which provided a disincentive to hire older workers. For example, one focus group participant told us that his prior employer had told him not to hire anyone older than him. In addition to increased health insurance costs, according to experts, workforce professionals, and our focus group participants, some employers may be hesitant to hire older workers because of the higher wages that many older workers earned in their previous jobs. Also, according to experts we interviewed, employers may believe that an older worker who previously held a high-level position will be overqualified and therefore unhappy in a lower-level position.

Another challenge that some older workers face in finding new jobs is that they may lack up-to-date computer skills. Some noted that after a long spell of unemployment, even those older workers who had previously been proficient with computer technology might find their technology skills outdated. Some experts we interviewed said that employers might hesitate to hire and retrain older workers because they assume that older workers will not want to work much longer, so the employer would not get a good return on the training investment.

According to workforce professionals, an ongoing trend among employers—to require job seekers to submit all applications and résumés online—creates difficulties for many older workers, particularly those with few or no computer skills. Further, workforce professionals told us that many online job applications require applicants to disclose information that readily reveals the applicant's age—such as the year the job seeker graduated from high school—and that applications cannot be submitted until such fields are completed. Workforce professionals also said that even workers seeking jobs that require little or no computer use could get those jobs only by completing a long online application. For example, workforce professionals told us that individuals seeking positions as maids and janitors in national chain hotels could apply for those positions only online and that the older workers seeking those positions were often unfamiliar with such applications.

Job Loss Can Lead to Lower Retirement Income

Job loss can result in fewer years of work over a worker's lifetime, which can lower the worker's retirement income in several ways. For example, fewer years of work can prevent a worker who is covered by a traditional DB plan from having enough years of work with an employer to vest in (that is, earn a nonforfeitable right to receive) employer-funded retirement benefits. And even if a worker who is covered by a traditional DB plan has enough years of work to earn a right to the benefits, fewer years of work can reduce a worker's final retirement benefit if the number of years worked is used in the formula for calculating retirement benefits. For workers with DC plans, having fewer years of work can limit the amount of yearly employee and employer contributions that accumulate in a worker's account. Moreover, Social Security retirement benefits may be reduced as a result of fewer years of work because the benefits are based, in part, on a calculation of the worker's average monthly earnings over 35 years. The 35 years used for the calculation are those with the worker's highest earnings, adjusted for changes in wage levels. If a worker has less than 35 years of earnings, then zeros would be used for earnings in the missing years, and this will result in a lower calculated benefit.

At the same time, long-term unemployment can motivate older workers to file for early Social Security retirement benefits. Many unemployed older workers in our focus groups said that they were planning to claim Social Security retirement benefits as soon as they were eligible or had already done so because they needed a source of income to help pay for living expenses. Moreover, a 2012 study found that high unemployment increases Social Security retirement claims among men with limited education. The spike in claims for Social Security retirement benefits that occurred in 2009 after large increases in unemployment rates offers support for the study's findings. According to estimates from SSA's Office of the Chief Actuary, in fiscal year 2009 about 139,500 (about 6 percent) more older workers applied for Social Security retirement benefits than would have been expected in the absence of a recession. Because Social Security retirement benefits claimed before full retirement age are reduced to account for the longer period of time that the benefits will be received, early claiming will cause individuals and their survivors to have lower monthly retirement benefits for the rest of their lives.

The recession also led to an increase in applications for disability benefits from the Social Security Disability Insurance program. In turn, the percentage of individuals in the population age 50 and over who have been awarded disability benefits has increased since the recession started. Older workers who lost their jobs in the recession and had significant injuries or health problems, and were not old enough to claim Social Security retirement benefits, have strong incentive to apply for Social Security disability benefits. If they are awarded benefits, they will receive monthly payments and, after a 24-month waiting period, they will be eligible for health insurance from the Medicare program. Also, receiving Social Security disability benefits gives unemployed older workers an alternative to claiming Social Security retirement benefits early.

Unemployed older workers who have a retirement account may also end up using some or all of those savings to cover living expenses while unemployed. Indeed, just over half of the older workers in our focus groups who reported having retirement savings in an IRA or a DC plan also reported that they had used some or all of these savings to pay for expenses while they were unemployed. More specifically, focus group participants described using retirement savings to cover expenses such as mortgage and car payments, medical bills, a child's college tuition, and moving to more affordable housing. A survey of unemployed workers conducted in March 2010 also found that a high percentage of individuals 55 and over reported using savings set aside for retirement or other purposes to help make ends meet. In addition, an October 2010 survey of workers age 50 and over found that nearly a quarter reported that they had used all their savings in the previous 3 years.

These recent developments are particularly troubling considering the fact that the earlier a worker stops working and cashes out DC plan savings, the lower the savings will be and the shorter the period that the savings are likely to last. Depending on the level of savings, the length of time the worker spends unemployed, and the worker's other financial resources, a worker may be at risk of using a large percentage of DC plan savings during unemployment. If, however, the worker is fortunate enough to find another job that includes an employer-sponsored retirement plan or pays enough to enable the worker to save some earnings in an IRA, the worker may be able to resume saving for retirement. . . .

Policy Options and Actions Taken to Help Unemployed Older Workers

Experts GAO interviewed selected various policies that have been proposed to help address unemployed older workers' reemployment challenges. Experts selected these policies from a broad list of policies that GAO compiled from previous academic studies. For example, two of the policies that experts selected would provide incentives such as temporary wage or training subsidies for employers to hire long-term unemployed older workers. Another policy experts selected would require long-term unemployed workers to enroll in training to remain eligible for unemployment insurance benefits. In the current context of high unemployment and slow job creation, the impact of such policies is likely to be muted by limited job openings.

In 2006, Labor convened an interagency Taskforce on the Aging of the American Workforce (the Taskforce), in part, in response to a request from this committee and its current chairman, Senator Herb Kohl. After the Taskforce issued its report in 2008, Labor implemented several strategies the report recommended. For example, in 2008, Labor expanded a demonstration project designed to assist individuals in creating or expanding their own businesses. Also, in 2009, Labor awarded approximately $10 million in grants to 10 organizations to test new ways of providing training and other services to connect older Americans with employment opportunities in high-growth, high-demand industries. According to Labor officials, the onset of the 2007–2009 recession shifted Labor's focus away from implementing strategies recommended in the Taskforce report to responding to greatly increased demand for services.

Concluding Observations

Although long-term unemployment hurts job seekers of all ages, it poses particular challenges for older workers. Older workers tend to be out of work longer than younger workers, threatening their retirement savings during a period of their lives when they have may have less opportunity to rebuild them. Even when they are able to obtain reemployment, they often do so at lower wages, making it even more difficult to replenish the lost earnings and reduced retirement savings that they suffered. For those long-term unemployed workers who cannot find work, they may leave the labor market altogether and claim Social Security retirement benefits earlier than they would have otherwise, leaving them with less retirement income each month for the rest of their lives. As such, the effects of the recent recession highlight the limitations of our current retirement security system.

While Labor took steps to implement some of the 2008 Taskforce recommendations, Labor officials understandably shifted their focus away from the report's findings when the recent recession caused a dramatic increase in demand for workforce services. Still, older workers remain a critical and growing segment of the workforce, and a renewed focus is now needed to identify strategies to help address older workers' significant reemployment challenges. In our report, we recommended that Labor consider what strategies are needed to address the unique needs of older job seekers, in light of recent economic and technological changes. In its comments on our draft report, Labor agreed with our recommendation.

> *"The [UN Population Fund] report urges governments to summon the political will to protect the elderly and ensure they can age with good health and dignity."*

Aging Populations Worldwide Should Have Strong Legal Protections

Elaine Kurtenbach

Elaine Kurtenbach is a reporter for the Associated Press. In the following viewpoint, she considers the findings of a 2012 United Nations Population Fund report, which urges governments around the world to find a way to ensure income security and access to essential health and social services for the world's aging population. The report finds that the elderly are often subject to age discrimination and suffer from high rates of poverty. Bold political leadership is needed to initiate open and useful policy discussions that will result in effective measures. One such measure would be, for example, strengthening social benefits and other safety nets for the aging.

As you read, consider the following questions:

1. According to a United Nations Population Fund report cited by Kurtenbach, how many countries will have 30 percent of their populations over age 60 by 2050?

2. As reported by the author, how many people in the world does the UN Population Fund estimate are 60 or older?

3. According to the UN Population Fund, as reported by Kurtenbach, how many people around the world suffered from dementia in 2010?

The fast aging of Japanese society is evident as soon as one lands at Tokyo's Narita airport and sees who is doing the cleaning. Young people tend to take such menial jobs in other countries, but here they are often held by workers obviously in the second half-century of their lives.

Addressing Aging Populations

Having the world's highest percentage of older people is creating unique challenges for Japan, but a report released Monday [October 1, 2012] by the U.N. Population Fund warns that they will not be unique for long. Japan is the only country with 30 percent of its population over 60, but by 2050 more than 60 other countries, from China to Canada to Albania, will be in the same boat.

The report urges governments to summon the political will to protect the elderly and ensure they can age with good health and dignity. Discrimination toward and poverty among the aged are still far too prevalent in many countries, it says, even in the relatively wealthy industrialized nations.

The problem is worse for women, whose access to jobs and health care is often limited throughout their lives, along with their rights to own and inherit property.

"More must be done to expose, investigate and prevent discrimination, abuse and violence against older persons, especially women who are more vulnerable," the report says, calling on countries to "ensure that aging is a time of opportunity for all."

"We need bold political leadership," said Babatunde Osotimehin, executive director of the Population Fund. "Aging is manageable, but first it must be managed."

Emerging Issues

In some countries, such as Latvia and Cyprus, about half of those over 60 are living in poverty. And even in highly industrialized countries such as Japan the elderly face problems that get little attention from the government.

Hisako Tsukida, a 77-year-old retired elementary school teacher in Japan's ancient capital of Kyoto, is living what sounds like a dream retirement life, taking tai chi and flower arrangement lessons and visiting a fitness center for spa treatments and muscle training.

But her current leisure followed many years of caring for her ailing husband and then for her mother. Japan's elderly often take on enormous burdens in caring for older relatives at home.

Tsukida spent years trying to find a nursing home for her mother, now 100, and finally succeeded about six months ago after a rare vacancy opened up. But now she wonders about the time when she'll have to go through the same struggle for herself.

"I wonder if I could do this again when I'm even older and need to find myself a place to go," she said.

Solutions Are Needed

The U.N. report said that policy discussions of all kinds must include a consideration of problems facing the aging if mankind is to reap a "longevity benefit" from people's longer life expectancies.

Who Is Old

The United Nations uses 60 years to refer to older people. This line, which divides younger and older cohorts of a population, is also used by demographers. However, in many developed countries, the age of 65 is used as a reference point for older persons as this is often the age at which persons become eligible for old-age social security benefits. So, there is no exact definition of "old" as this concept has different meanings in different societies.

Defining "old" is further challenged by the changing average lifespan of human beings. . . .

There are other definitions of "old" that go beyond chronological age. Old age as a social construct is often associated with a change of social roles and activities, for example, becoming a grandparent or a pensioner. Older persons often define old age as a stage at which functional, mental and physical capacity is declining and people are more prone to disease or disabilities.

Discussions with older people in South Africa, for example, showed that they associated old age both with experience gained in life and increasing dependence on others. Chronological definitions of old age were not viewed as so important in signifying old age as changes in physical and mental capacity.

Older persons are a highly diverse population group, in terms of, for example, age, sex, ethnicity, education, income and health. It is important to recognize this in order to adequately address the needs of all older persons, especially the most vulnerable.

United Nations Population Fund,
"Ageing in the Twenty-First Century:
A Celebration and a Challenge," 2012.

Governments should build safety nets to ensure older people have income security and access to essential health and social services, it said. The report cited data from the International Labor Organization showing that only about a fifth of all workers get comprehensive social insurance.

Aging is no longer solely an issue for rich countries. About two-thirds of people over 60 years old live in developing countries such as China, and by 2050 that figure is expected to rise to about 80 percent.

One in nine people—810 million—are 60 or older, a figure projected to rise to one in five—or more than 2 billion—by 2050.

Japan's Challenge

Even Japan, the world's third-largest economy, offers only meager social benefits, though government-subsidized services provide affordable household help and daycare in some areas.

Neighbors and religious groups often help older people, and public facilities have been vastly improved from a few decades ago, with elevators and other handicapped access now the norm.

The discovery earlier this year, though, that an aged couple and their son apparently had starved to death in their home in a Tokyo suburb highlighted Japan's own growing problems with poverty and unemployment.

Growing numbers of people suffering from dementia pose another challenge. About 35.6 million people around the world were afflicted with the disease in 2010, a number growing about 7.7 million a year and costing about $604 billion worldwide.

Provisions must be made for the infirm to ensure their basic human rights, the U.N. report says.

Bias Toward Youth

In many countries, including the United States, India, Brazil and Mexico, statistics show the elderly often pay more into pension systems over their lifetimes than they receive in return. Meanwhile, as retirement ages are raised and benefits cut due to ballooning deficits, the elderly are paying proportionately more in taxes.

The report blamed a bias toward youth in mass media, which stereotype aging as a time of decline, for lowering expectations about life for older people. It noted that older people often live highly productive, enjoyable lives if they have good health and reasonable levels of income.

The report's authors also argued against a prevalent belief that older workers should make way for younger job seekers, saying that way of thinking is based on the mistaken idea that there is a finite number of jobs and that workers are perfectly interchangeable.

"More jobs for older people do not mean fewer jobs for younger people," it says.

> *"The problem is that—lacking the Driv-*
> *ing Miss Daisy option—there's no clear*
> *personal, societal, or policy solution for*
> *what to do about older drivers."*

States Must Address the Issue of Aging Drivers

Emily Yoffe

Emily Yoffe is a regular contributor to Slate. *In the following viewpoint, she maintains that as America's population ages, there will be more and more elderly drivers on the road. There needs to be a coherent and effective strategy to deal with the is-sue of aging, impaired drivers, including imposing restrictions on licensing. Yoffe notes that many states already do have measures in place to frequently test the driving ability of aging drivers to screen out those who can no longer drive safely. Families need to find ways to sensitively and effectively deal with aging drivers in order to protect them and others out on the road, she concludes.*

As you read, consider the following questions:

1. According to the Insurance Institute for Highway Safety (IIHS), as cited by Yoffe, how many licensed drivers aged 70 and older were there in 2008?

2. How many traffic fatalities were there in 2010, according to the author?

3. According to the IIHS, as reported by Yoffe, how many fewer miles per year do the elderly drive compared to middle-aged drivers?

Last fall, Gordon Yeager, 94, and his wife, Norma, 90, died together, holding hands in the Iowa hospital where they had been taken after a car accident. The final chapter of the couple's seven-decade love story made headlines around the world. What the fulsome tributes to the couple's 72-year marriage generally failed to note was that the crash nearly ended another long love story. The Yeagers lost their lives after Gordon failed to obey a stop sign and plowed into the car of Charles and Barbara Clapsaddle, who have been married for 38 years. Charles was uninjured, but Barbara's neck was broken. Fortunately, she can still walk. After a long hospitalization and rehabilitation, she has returned home where she slowly continues to recover.

The collision had all the hallmarks of a car accident caused by an aged driver. When old people are involved in fatal crashes, the Insurance Institute for Highway Safety reports, their victims are most likely to be themselves and their equally elderly, frail passengers. Intersections are particularly perilous. According to a study in the journal *Traffic Injury Prevention*, intersection crashes accounted for about one half of the fatalities in accidents among drivers 85 and older. The study found that when drivers 70 to 79 were involved in intersection collisions they tended to misjudge whether it was safe to proceed. Those 80 and over simply failed to see the other car.

Our Aging Population

As the boomers head toward senescence, the old will account for a growing percentage of the population, and thus an increasing proportion of people on the road. Most elderly

Americans will end their lives with a valid driver's license in their wallets. According to the IIHS, there were 22 million licensed drivers aged 70 and older as of 2008, representing 78 percent of that demographic group. The problem is that—lacking the *Driving Miss Daisy* [a movie about an elderly woman and her chauffeur] option—there's no clear personal, societal, or policy solution for what to do about older drivers. As many children of elderly parents know, it can be agonizingly hard to get older drivers who are no longer competent to hand over their keys.

The stories of the carnage caused by unfit older drivers are sobering. There was 86-year-old George Weller, who drove through the Santa Monica farmer's market in 2003, killing 10 and injuring 63. Two years ago, an 81-year-old Florida woman failed to yield when merging onto the highway, smashing into a bus carrying seniors on an elder hostel trip, killing at least two and injuring dozens.

Despite these dreadful incidents, it's wrong to assume that our streets are about to become the setting for the Cataract 500. Though the toll remains enormous, a fortunate trend over the past 40 years is that the roads are safer for everyone, with a national decline in traffic fatalities from a high of 54,600 in 1972 to about 33,800 in 2010. The reasons for the improvement are numerous, from a crackdown on drunk driving, to safer car design, to seatbelt laws, to the introduction of graduated licensing for teens. Older drivers, too, are less likely to be involved in traffic fatalities than in years past, with recent evidence showing a welcome and unexpected falloff.

Anne McCartt, senior vice president for research at the IIHS, says older drivers are often unfairly demonized. For one thing, they are less likely than other groups to speed and drive drunk. And no group of drivers is more hazardous than teenagers, with their combination of inexperience and recklessness. But while teens mature and become safer, increasing maturity has the opposite effect on the old. Once people turn 70, their crash rates start to tick up. After 80, the acceleration is marked. Octogenarians on up have a higher collision rate per mile traveled of any age group except for teens, and their rate of fatal collisions per mile traveled is the highest of all drivers.

Current Restrictions on Older Drivers

More than one half of U.S. states impose restrictions on license renewals for older drivers. In Alaska, drivers 69 and older must renew in person, not by mail. The District of Columbia requires a fitness-to-drive statement from a physician starting at age 70. In Illinois, those 75 and over must take a road test. In Iowa, where Yeager lived, the renewal cycle is accelerated from every five years to every two years for drivers 70 and above. McCartt says studies on the effectiveness of these screening procedures have been mixed and that there is no certain way to identify the highest risk driver. "For most states, and most people in highway safety, the goal would be keeping older people driving as safely and as long as they can. Taking a license away is a major thing to do. It has a big effect on mobility and independence and states need good evidence before they impose this." Motor vehicle administrators can also issue licenses with specific restrictions. For example, drivers can be confined to a certain number of miles from their home, or even allowed to travel only to church or the grocery store.

As older drivers decline physically or cognitively, many do loosen their grip on the wheel voluntarily. The IIHS reports that those 70 and over drive less than half as many miles annually as middle-aged drivers. Numerous studies show that many older people restrict their time on the road by no longer driving at night, avoiding freeways, or staying home during bad weather. My father-in-law died at 98 with a valid driver's license (it expired on his 100th birthday), but he didn't get behind the wheel for at least the last five years of his life. After

Environmental Changes Can Improve Safety for Older Drivers

Much can be done to improve roadway safety for all drivers, but especially for seniors. Improving the visibility of road signs and pavement markings through lettering, size or color can be particularly important for older drivers who may have visual impairments. . . . Intersections are a particular problem for older drivers, and countermeasures may include adding left-turn lanes and left-turn traffic signals. One study found that low-cost modifications to intersections (e.g., making traffic signals more visible, adding a dedicated left-turn lane) resulted in a 13 percent greater reduction in injury crashes per licensed driver for drivers 65 and older compared with drivers ages 25–64.

Another approach is to reconfigure existing or new intersections as roundabouts, which reduce vehicle speeds and eliminate some of the most complicated aspects of traditional intersections. In a study of intersections that were converted from stop signs or traffic signals to roundabouts, injury crashes were reduced by 76 percent. However, older drivers favor roundabouts somewhat less than younger drivers. In surveys taken at least one year after the construction of new roundabouts in six communities, 65 percent of drivers ages 65 and older favored the roundabouts, compared with 70 percent of drivers 35–64 and 74 percent of drivers 18–34. No studies have focused on the effects of roundabouts on crashes among older drivers, who may find them difficult to navigate.

"Q&A: Older Drivers,"
Insurance Institute of Highway Safety,
September 2012. www.iihs.org.

a series of conversations with his children about their concerns that he was getting too frail to drive, he finally conceded it was time.

Going Rogue

That's the ideal—self-recognition and the support of loving family leading the older person to accept it's the end of the road. The AARP's suitably depressing multimedia guide, titled "We Need to Talk," envisions such a world, one in which seniors quickly move from resentment that their driving skills are being impugned to gratitude that their children care. But many old people do not go gentle into calling a cab. When rational discussion fails, the Hartford insurance company suggests Stuxnet-style subterfuge: disable the car, file down the keys, and cancel the vehicle registration. Even then, after a lifetime of being law-abiding, the company acknowledges elderly motorists may go rogue: "Drivers may continue to drive without a driver's license, car registration, or insurance coverage."

This is the situation a woman, who asks to be called Lu, finds herself in with her father-in-law, let's call him Roger. Lu and her husband live in Houston, while 83-year-old Roger lives near Dallas. Though Roger and his wife reside in a retirement community that provides a van for residents, Roger insists on having his own car. He insists despite the fact that his last arrest for drunk driving resulted in the suspension of his license by the state and the confiscation of his car by his son. One day, Lu's husband—let's call him Dave—got a call from the manager of the retirement community. She thought he'd want to know that his father had just turned up driving a white Chevy Cobalt. Dave flew up, checked into a motel, and hired a tow truck to haul the used car back to the dealership.

There was just one problem: Dave had towed the wrong dinged and dented Cobalt, one that belonged to another resident. Dave had the other Cobalt towed back, but then he had to leave for a conference. The upshot is that Roger is still driving. The family does have a radical option not available for most elderly drivers: They could notify the judge who presided over Roger's license suspension, which would land him back in jail. But his sons are afraid that would kill Roger. "He's been told over and over what the full ramifications are of his driving, and he understands," says Lu. "We just live with our fingers crossed."

Sometimes the problem is that the older parent is drifting away mentally, and facing this loss is just too painful for everyone. Writer Nancy Palmer's mother, then in her 70s, was increasingly forgetful and had gotten lost driving home a few times. The family took her in for an evaluation and raised the possibility of taking away her license. "But she said the most poignant thing," Palmer recalls. "She said, 'I've been driving since I was 16.'" So the family backed off.

One morning Palmer's mother got in her Volkswagen Golf, went to the gas station to fill the car, and disappeared. At midnight, the frantic family got a call from the police two counties away. They had spotted Palmer's mother driving erratically. She refused to stop when a police car approached with a bullhorn. Finally, the officers blew out her tires with spike strips. That was the end. Palmer's mother continued to ask for her car keys but her children told her the car was too damaged to drive.

A Physician's Role

Grown children who struggle to get their parents to hand over the keys can turn to the parents' physician to help. But for one middle-aged woman, her 85-year-old father's doctor turned out to be another roadblock. The woman's father, who lives in Maryland, suffers from advanced Parkinson's and freezes while behind the wheel, but he insists on driving himself to visit his wife, who's in a nursing home. She begged her father's doctor to report him to the state's motor vehicle department. The doctor, though, said he'd only send a letter if the father agreed, which he defiantly did not. "It seems that the whole system is biased toward the rights of the driver, not the right of the public to be safe," she says.

It turns out only a handful of states require physicians to report such impaired drivers, though in most states doctors who reach out to the motor vehicle department are protected from liability by a good faith exemption. The chief of the medical advisory board of Maryland's Motor Vehicle Administration, former trauma surgeon Carl Soderstrom, would like to see physicians think about their patient's fitness to drive as part of a health assessment. While doctors in Maryland have no legal obligation to report unfit elderly drivers, Soderstrom says "we believe you have a moral obligation."

The Difficulty of Dealing with Older Drivers

Gordon Yeager was one of those old drivers who just refused to get the message, and his story illustrates how difficult it is to take away the license of someone who's determined to keep it, even in a state like Iowa with a strong monitoring program. Not that his son, Dennis, 52, was overly concerned. "I would ride with him to breakfast once in a while," he said in an interview. "Truthfully, he gets older and you wonder. A car would come up, and I was thinking, 'Is he going to stop?' But he did really good."

When Yeager showed up last Oct. 7 at his local motor vehicle division, the condition of the 94-year-old concerned the employees. He was told he needed to take a road test. He failed. In Iowa, flunking drivers are given a suspension notice and a temporary permit—they have 30 days to retake the test and can do so as many as three times. So Yeager drove home, planning to try again. Dennis Yeager says his father told him he was "set up." The elder Yeager claimed that at an intersection the examiner instructed him to get into a right-turn-only lane, then ordered him to drive straight. "That is not possible," says Kim Snook, director of the office of driver services for the Iowa Department of Transportation. "Never have we used tricks to fail someone." Five days later, Yeager and his wife were dead after crashing into the Clapsaddles' Mustang.

Charles Clapsaddle, 65, is now caring for his wife Barbara, 60, who has racked up more than $250,000 in medical bills. He says of their ordeal, "We're not bitter. We're unhappy the other couple was killed. But they should not have been out driving anyway."

Periodical and Internet Sources Bibliography

The following articles have been selected to supplement the diverse views presented in this chapter.

Curt Burnett	"Age Discrimination Is a Growing Issue in a Difficult Economy," *Deseret News*, March 8, 2012.
Jane Gross	"Should Doctors Stop Patients from Driving?" *New York Times*, February 22, 2011.
Michael Kinsley	"Kept Down by the (Young) Man," *Los Angeles Times*, March 23, 2012.
Jessica Lappin	"Code Word for Age Discrimination," *The Huffington Post*, January 17, 2013.
Michele Merens	"Ageism Hinders Some Job Seekers," *Milwaukee Journal Sentinel*, January 24, 2013. www.jsonline.com.
Christopher Middleton	"Who Says It's the End of the Road for Elderly Drivers?" *The Telegraph*, March 12, 2012.
Joshua Rhett Miller	"Diminished Motor Skills: 'Silver Tsunami' of Elderly Drivers Prompts Tough Decisions," Fox News, April 16, 2012.
N.V.	"Difference Engine: End of the Road," *The Economist*, October 29, 2012.
Bernard Perusse	"Rock of Ageism," *Montreal Gazette*, November 23, 2012.
Graham Snowdon	"Young and Older People 'Experience Age Discrimination at Work," *The Guardian*, January 16, 2012.
Steve Tobak	"Dark Side of Social Media: Age Discrimination," CBS News, January 31, 2012.

OPPOSING
VIEWPOINTS®
SERIES

Is Social Security Viable and Effective for an Aging Population?

Chapter Preface

The establishment of the Social Security program can be traced to the outbreak of the Great Depression in 1929, a period of great global economic hardship. In the United States, the economic crisis had terrible consequences for many people, especially the poor and elderly. For older Americans, the rates of poverty skyrocketed. By 1934 over half of the elderly in America could not support themselves financially. During those lean years of the Great Depression, elderly below the poverty level lived with family and relied on financial support from family, friends, or charity. Those that didn't have access to such resources suffered greatly.

In an attempt to help elderly Americans, many states began to pass legislation to create welfare pensions for qualified citizens in the 1930s. By 1935 thirty states had some form of old-age pension program. The problem was that these state pension programs reached too few people and provided too little compensation. According to the Social Security Administration, only about 3 percent of the elderly received benefits, and the average benefit amount was about 65 cents a day.

Clearly there was a need for a federal program to help the nation's elderly from falling into poverty. Government reformers found inspiration in the social insurance movement, an intellectual tradition originating in nineteenth-century Europe that posited that the government was responsible for the economic security of its citizens. On June 8, 1934, President Franklin D. Roosevelt announced his intention to create a program for the social security of America's older population. He created the Committee on Economic Security, a working group of five cabinet-level officials, to research the problem and formulate a series of recommendations for such a program. The committee produced a comprehensive study in January 1935 that became the basis of the Social Security program.

On August 14, 1935, President Roosevelt signed the Social Security Act into law. Social Security was created to be a social insurance program that paid retired workers (age 65 or older) a regular income, as well as provide benefits for other groups in need of income security. At the signing, President Roosevelt noted that the law was beneficial not only to the individuals and families depending on it, but also for the country's economic future. "We can never insure one hundred percent of the population against one hundred percent of the hazards and vicissitudes of life, but we have tried to frame a law which will give some measure of protection to the average citizen and to his family against the loss of a job and against poverty-ridden old age," he asserted. "This law, too, represents a cornerstone in a structure which is being built but is by no means complete. It is a structure intended to lessen the force of possible future depressions. It will act as a protection to future Administrations against the necessity of going deeply into debt to furnish relief to the needy. The law will flatten out the peaks and valleys of deflation and of inflation. It is, in short, a law that will take care of human needs and at the same time provide the United States an economic structure of vastly greater soundness."

The following chapter examines the viability and effectiveness of Social Security in the twenty-first century. Viewpoints included in this section focus on the efficacy and popularity of the program, accusations that Social Security is a Ponzi scheme, and questions about the program's future.

"Social Security provides a foundation of retirement protection for people at all earnings levels."

Social Security Is a Popular and Effective Program

Center on Budget and Policy Priorities

The Center on Budget and Policy Priorities is a public policy organization that focuses on fiscal policy. In the following viewpoint, the Center lauds Social Security as one of the country's most successful, effective, and popular public policy programs. The American people support Social Security because it is not just a retirement program, but a life insurance and disability insurance program as well. It offers a strong foundation of retirement protection for almost every American and is essential in the effort to keep elderly Americans out of poverty. The Center notes that Social Security is particularly important for minority groups and for women.

As you read, consider the following questions:

1. Which US president signed Social Security into law in 1935?

Center on Budget and Policy Priorities, "Policy Basics: Top Ten Facts About Social Security," November 6, 2012. Copyright © 2012 by The Center on Budget and Policy Priorities. All rights reserved. Reproduced by permission.

2. According to the author, how many Americans collected Social Security benefits in June 2012?

3. What was the average Social Security retirement benefit in June 2012, according to the author?

President Franklin Roosevelt signed the Social Security Act on August 14, 1935. Almost eight decades later, Social Security remains one of the nation's most successful, effective, and popular programs. It provides a foundation of income on which workers can build to plan for their retirement. It also provides valuable social insurance protection to workers who become disabled and to families whose breadwinner dies.

Fact #1: Social Security is more than just a retirement program. It provides important life insurance and disability insurance protection as well.

In June 2012, 56 million people, or about one in every six U.S. residents, collected Social Security benefits. While three-quarters of them received benefits as retirees or elderly widow(er)s, another 11 million (19 percent) received disability insurance benefits, and 2 million (4 percent) received benefits as young survivors of deceased workers.

Workers earn life insurance and disability insurance protection by making Social Security payroll tax contributions:

About 96 percent of people aged 20–49 who worked in jobs covered by Social Security in 2011 have earned life insurance protection through Social Security. For a young worker with average earnings, a spouse, and two children, that Social Security protection is equivalent to a life insurance policy with a face value of $476,000. About 91 percent of people aged 21–64 who worked in covered employment in 2011 are insured through Social Security in case of disability.

The risk of disability or premature death is greater than many people realize. Of recent entrants to the labor force, almost four in ten men (37 percent) and three in ten women (31 percent) will become disabled or die before reaching the full retirement age.

Fact #2: Social Security provides a guaranteed, progressive benefit that keeps up with increases in the cost of living.

Social Security benefits are based on the earnings on which you pay Social Security payroll taxes. The higher are your earnings (up to a maximum taxable amount, currently $110,100 and slated to rise automatically to $113,700 in 2013), the higher will be your benefit.

Social Security benefits are progressive: they represent a higher proportion of a worker's previous earnings for workers at lower earnings levels. For example, benefits for someone who earned about 45 percent of the average wage and then retired at age 65 in 2012 replace about 55 percent of his or her prior earnings. But benefits for a person who always earned the maximum taxable amount replace only 27 percent of his or her prior earnings, though they are larger in dollar terms than those for the lower-wage worker.

In recent years, fewer employers have offered defined-benefit pension plans, which guarantee a certain benefit level upon retirement, and more have offered defined-*contribution* plans, which pay a benefit based on a worker's contributions and the rate of return they earn. Thus, for most workers, Social Security will be their only source of guaranteed retirement income that is not subject to investment risk or financial market fluctuations.

Once someone starts receiving Social Security, his or her benefits automatically increase each year to keep pace with inflation, helping to ensure that people do not fall into poverty as they age. In contrast, most private pensions and annuities are not adjusted for inflation or are only partly adjusted.

Fact #3: Social Security provides a foundation of retirement protection for nearly every American, and its benefits are not means-tested.

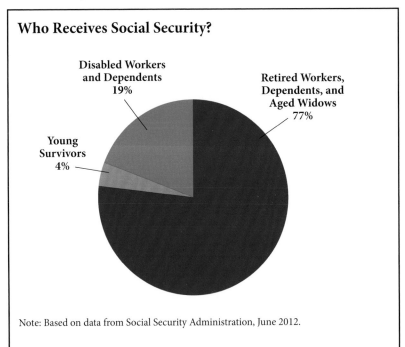

Who Receives Social Security?

Disabled Workers
and Dependents
19%

Young
Survivors
4%

Retired Workers,
Dependents, and
Aged Widows
77%

Note: Based on data from Social Security Administration, June 2012.

TAKEN FROM: Center on Budget and Policy Priorities, "Policy Basics: Top Ten Facts About Social Security," November 6, 2012. www.cbpp.org

Almost all workers participate in Social Security by making payroll tax contributions, and almost all elderly people receive Social Security benefits. The near-universality of Social Security brings many important advantages.

Social Security provides a foundation of retirement protection for people at all earnings levels. It encourages private pensions and personal saving because it isn't means-tested—in other words, it doesn't reduce or deny benefits to people if their current income or assets exceed a certain level. Social Security provides a higher annual payout for a dollar contributed than private retirement annuities because the risk pool is not limited to those who expect to live a long time, no funds leak out in lump-sum payments or bequests, and its administrative costs are much lower.

Indeed, universal participation and the absence of means-testing make Social Security very efficient to administer. Administrative costs amount to only 0.9 percent of annual benefits, far below the percentages for private retirement annuities. Proposals to means-test Social Security would undercut many of those important advantages.

Finally, the universal nature of Social Security assures its continued popular and political support. Large majorities of Americans say that they don't mind paying for Social Security because they value it for themselves, their families, and millions of others who rely on it.

Fact #4: Social Security benefits are modest.

Social Security benefits are much more modest than many people realize. In June 2012, the average Social Security retirement benefit was $1,234 a month, or about $14,800 a year. (The average disabled worker and aged widow received slightly less.) For someone who worked all of his or her adult life at average earnings and retires at 65 in 2012, Social Security benefits replace about 41 percent of past earnings. This "replacement rate" will slip to about 36 percent for a medium earner retiring at 65 in the future, chiefly because the full retirement age, which has already risen to 66, will climb to 67 over the 2017–2022 period.

Moreover, most retirees enroll in Medicare's Supplementary Medical Insurance (also known as Medicare Part B) and have Part B premiums deducted from their Social Security checks. As health-care costs continue to outpace general inflation, those premiums will take a bigger bite out of their checks.

Social Security benefits are modest by international standards, too. The United States ranks 30th among 34 developed countries in the percentage of a median worker's earnings that the public-pension system replaces.

Fact #5: Children have an important stake in Social Security.

Social Security is important for children and their families as well as for the elderly.

About 6 million children under age 18 (8 percent of all U.S. children) lived in families that received income from Social Security in 2011. That number included over 3 million children who received their own benefits as dependents of retired, disabled, or deceased workers, as well as others who lived with parents or relatives who received Social Security benefits.

Social Security lifted 1.1 million children out of poverty in 2011.

Fact #6: Almost half of the elderly would be poor without Social Security. Social Security lifts 14 million elderly Americans out of poverty.

Without Social Security benefits, more than 40 percent of Americans aged 65 and older would have incomes below the federal poverty line, all else being equal. With Social Security benefits, less than one-tenth of the elderly do. The program lifts 14 million elderly Americans out of poverty. Almost 90 percent of people aged 65 or older receive some income from Social Security. Those not receiving Social Security mostly comprise recent immigrants, state and local government retirees (and federal retirees hired before 1984) who are covered by separate retirement systems, people under age 66 with significant earnings, and people who are so seriously disabled that they never worked and also have never married.

Fact #7: Most elderly beneficiaries rely on Social Security for the majority of their income.

For nearly two-thirds (65 percent) of elderly beneficiaries, Social Security provides the majority of their cash income. For more than one-third (36 percent), it provides more than 90 percent of their income. For one-quarter (24 percent) of elderly beneficiaries, Social Security is the sole source of retirement income.

Reliance on Social Security increases with age, as older people are less likely to work and more likely to have depleted their savings. Among those aged 80 or older, Social Security provides the majority of income for 76 percent of beneficiaries and nearly all of the income for 45 percent of beneficiaries.

Fact #8: Social Security is particularly important for minorities.

Social Security is a particularly important source of income for groups with low earnings and with less opportunity to save and earn pensions, including African Americans and Hispanics. Among beneficiaries aged 65 and older, Social Security represents 90 percent or more of income for 35 percent of elderly white beneficiaries, 42 percent of Asian Americans, 49 percent of blacks, and 55 percent of Hispanics.

Blacks and Hispanics benefit substantially from Social Security because, on average, they have higher rates of disability and lower lifetime earnings than whites. Hispanics also have longer average life expectancies than whites, which means that they have more years to collect retirement benefits. Blacks are much more likely to benefit from survivors insurance. In 2010, African Americans made up 12.6 percent of the population, but 23 percent of children receiving Social Security survivor benefits were African American.

Fact #9: Social Security is especially beneficial for women.

Because women tend to earn less than men, take more time out of the paid workforce, live longer, accumulate less savings, and receive smaller pensions, Social Security is especially important for them. Women constitute 56 percent of Social Security beneficiaries aged 62 and older and 67 percent of beneficiaries aged 85 and older.

Women pay 41 percent of Social Security payroll taxes but receive nearly half of Social Security benefits. This is because women benefit disproportionately from the program's inflation-protected benefits (because women tend to live longer), its progressive formula for computing benefits (because they tend to have lower earnings), and its benefits for non-working spouses and survivors.

Fact #10: Social Security can pay full benefits through 2033 without any changes. Relatively modest changes would place the program on a sound financial footing for 75 years and beyond.

Social Security's costs will grow in coming years as members of the large Baby Boom generation (those born between 1946 and 1964) move into their retirement years. Since the mid-1980s, however, Social Security has collected more in taxes and other income each year than it pays out in benefits and has amassed combined trust funds of $2.7 trillion, invested in interest-bearing Treasury securities. The trust funds will enable Social Security to keep paying full benefits through 2033 without any changes in the program, even though one of the two funds, the Disability Insurance (DI) trust fund, faces exhaustion in 2016. (The much bigger Old-Age and Survivors Insurance trust fund would last until 2035. Combined, the two funds would be exhausted in 2033.) Policymakers should address DI's pending depletion in the context of action on overall Social Security solvency. If they are unable to agree on a sensible solvency package in time, however, they should reallocate revenues between the two trust funds, as they have often done in the past.

After 2033, when the combined trust funds will be exhausted if no changes are made, Social Security would still be able [to] pay three-fourths of its scheduled benefits using its annual tax revenue. Alarmists who claim that Social Security won't be around when today's young workers retire either misunderstand or misrepresent the projections.

The long-term gap between Social Security's projected income and promised benefits is estimated at 1 percent of gross domestic product (GDP) over the next 75 years (and 1.5 percent of GDP in 2086). By coincidence, that only slightly exceeds the revenue loss over the next 75 years from extending the Bush tax cuts for people making over $250,000.

Letting the tax cuts expire would not "pay for" fixing Social Security, which has different sources of revenues; conversely, letting them continue would not directly harm Social Security. Nevertheless, members of Congress cannot simultaneously claim that the tax cuts for the richest 2 percent of Americans are affordable while the Social Security shortfall constitutes a dire fiscal threat.

A mix of tax increases and modest benefit reductions—carefully crafted to shield the neediest recipients and give ample notice to all participants—could put the program on a sound financial footing indefinitely. As Social Security approaches its 80th birthday, policymakers have an opportunity to reassure future generations that they, too, can count on this successful program.

> *"Advocates of Social Security ... point to its original intent of providing 'old-age insurance.' But Social Security does a very poor job today of fulfilling this function."*

Social Security Is an Ineffective Program

Jagadeesh Gokhale

Jagadeesh Gokhale is a senior fellow at the Cato Institute, a public policy research organization dedicated to the principles of individual liberty and limited government. In the following viewpoint, he states that Social Security is an ineffective government program that fails to produce anything of value. Most importantly, he claims, the program's various retributive features do not offer effective social insurance because it does little to change the distribution of economic well-being. Gokhale believes that Social Security also discourages lower-income households from saving for retirement, which means less money passed on to later generations. In addition, he contends, Social Security does a poor job of providing effective old-age insurance. Gokhale maintains that there needs to be an honest and open discussion about the problems of Social Security, devoid of inaccuracies, distortions, and unsupportable claims.

As you read, consider the following questions:

1. What US governor and 2012 presidential candidate called Social Security a "Ponzi scheme"?

2. How does Gokhale describe a Ponzi scheme?

3. During what decade was Social Security's full retirement age set, according to the author?

Presidential candidate Governor Rick Perry's claim that Social Security is a "Ponzi scheme"—that is, the program not very different from the operation run by Bernard Madoff[1]—sparked a firestorm, but the comparison is not wholly inappropriate. Even so, that is [the] wrong issue to focus on. We've inherited a Social Security system which has survived court challenges, along with its unfunded liabilities—regardless of the fact that Social Security's primary transactions resemble that of a Ponzi scheme.

The question is what are we going to do about it in our time—sustain it or get rid of it? And, in both cases, how?

Ponzi Schemes

Many economists, including some Nobel laureates, have alluded to Social Security as a Ponzi scheme—one that takes money from new investors to directly pay to older investors as a return. As long as the population of investors keeps growing, the money coming in is sufficient to provide a positive rate of return to earlier investors. Eventually, however, the population of new investors must stop growing—at which point, investors cannot be repaid and the entire scheme collapses.

Using the "Ponzi scheme" label to describe such ventures in the private sector is legitimate. But what about when such ventures are operated by the government—such as Social Se-

---

1. Bernard Madoff is a former investment advisor who was convicted of fraud in 2009. Investors lost billions of dollars in the Ponzi scheme.

curity? Full disclosure: In 1996, I co-wrote an Economic Commentary for the Cleveland Federal Reserve, essentially comparing Social Security to a Ponzi scheme. I still agree with much of what it says although, in hindsight, I would express some of its ideas differently today.

A key test of whether Social Security is exactly like a Ponzi scheme—ignoring for the moment that it's operated by a sovereign—is whether it produces anything of value. It's supposed to produce value by providing "social insurance." What is that, exactly?

Social Security as Social Insurance

Advocates of sustaining Social Security's current structure (as opposed to its objectives of providing economic security to retirees and associated individuals) claim that it more efficiently provides support for those who suffer economic misfortunes during their lifetimes. Another description is that Social Security enables the pooling of economic risks across generations through its benefit formula that averages across high and low productivity experiences of different worker generations.

These advocates are wrong. In the last chapter of my book [*Social Security: A Fresh Look at Policy Alternatives*], I examine whether Social Security reduces the variability of lifetime incomes across people from what it would be without it. I find a very small negative effect of the program on cohort-specific variance of lifetime income, most of it arising from payroll taxes and very little from the benefit side of Social Security. That suggests that the program's various redistributive features do little to alter the distribution of economic well being. Other studies also refute the idea that Social Security is successful in providing social insurance through its redistributive provisions. In yet another study, I show how Social Security's current rules can prevent people from becoming richer over generations. Social Security's rules induce low income house-

Traditional Sources of Economic Security

All peoples throughout all of human history have faced the uncertainties brought on by unemployment, illness, disability, death and old age. In the realm of economics, these inevitable facets of life are said to be threats to one's *economic security*.

For the ancient Greeks economic security took the form of amphorae of olive oil. Olive oil was very nutritious and could be stored for relatively long periods. To provide for themselves in times of need the Greeks stockpiled olive oil and this was their form of economic security.

In medieval Europe, the feudal system was the basis of economic security, with the feudal lord responsible for the economic survival of the serfs working on the estate. The feudal lord had economic security as long as there was a steady supply of serfs to work the estate, and the serfs had economic security only so long as they were fit enough to provide their labor. . . .

Family members and relatives have always felt some degree of responsibility to one another, and to the extent that the family had resources to draw upon, this was often a source of economic security, especially for the aged or infirm. And land itself was an important form of economic security for those who owned it or who lived on farms.

These then are the traditional sources of economic security: assets; labor; family; and charity.

Social Security Administration, "Historical Background and Development of Social Security," 2012. www.ssa.gov.

holds to save very little through retirement, thereby preventing them bequeathing wealth to their children—unlike children of rich families.

Social Security as Old-Age Insurance

Advocates of Social Security also point to its original intent of providing "old-age insurance." But Social Security does a very poor job today of fulfilling this function. Living beyond Social Security's "full retirement age" of 66 is a relatively sure bet for 20-year-olds today compared to the 1930s when the program's full retirement age was set. Today, Social Security acts more as a "retirement saving" program than an "old-age insurance" program and its merits as a "productive business"—as opposed to a forced saving mechanism that doesn't actually result in higher national saving—should be seriously questioned. To restore its old-age insurance function to earlier levels, its retirement, survivor, and other benefit eligibility ages would have to be increased by significantly more than the scheduled increases enacted by Congress in 1983, which are currently underway.

Even with the results from the studies cited, actuaries' and economists' knowledge about how Social Security operates, how it affects the economy, and how it will evolve in the future is still quite limited, in view of the myriad factors influencing its finances. The public debate on Social Security is mired in inaccuracies, untrue factoids, unsupportable claims, and diversions into immaterial discussions, partly, but not exclusively, due to this imperfect information. That's unlikely [to] change anytime soon. The program will continue to bumble along until—like a Ponzi scheme—it doesn't.

"The complaints about Social Security are accurate: The only reason it has enjoyed such 'success' thus far is that it relied on increasing contributions from each new generation of workers."

Social Security Is a Ponzi Scheme

Robert P. Murphy

Robert P. Murphy is an author, blogger, and an adjunct scholar of the Mises Institute, an educational organization dedicated to research and teaching in the Austrian School of economics and political economy. The institute defends individual liberty, the free market, private property, sound money, and peace. In the following viewpoint, Murphy contends that Social Security is basically a Ponzi scheme because it takes funds from existing contributors to pay retirees no longer paying into the system. Social Security is unsustainable because there are more retirees receiving benefits and fewer workers putting money into the program. Private-sector retirement planning is much better than Social Security, he claims, because it encourages individuals to save more and invest wisely for retirement.

As you read, consider the following questions:

1. According to Murphy, what two Nobel-winning economists have both compared Social Security to a Ponzi scheme?

2. What object does the Social Security Administration use to visualize how Social Security works, as cited by the author?

3. What does Murphy describe as analogous to Social Security?

Ever since [governor and 2012 presidential candidate] Rick Perry derided Social Security as a Ponzi scheme, economists and other pundits have jumped into the fray. Progressive blogger Matt Yglesias says it's "nuts" for anyone to talk like this, because Social Security merely relies on future economic growth—just like a private pension plan. Free-market economist Alex Tabarrok responded to Yglesias with links to arch-Keynesians (and Nobel laureates) Paul Samuelson and Paul Krugman, both comparing Social Security to a "Ponzi game."

In the present [viewpoint] I have three aims: First, I will point out that the critics are right; to the extent that Social Security "worked," it was because of its resemblance to a classic Ponzi scheme. Second, I will show how private-sector retirement planning operates nothing like this. Third, I will defend the good name of Charles Ponzi from the scurrilous comparisons—what he did was nothing like the racket known as Social Security.

Social Security's "Ponzi Game Aspect"

Paul Krugman is a famous guy with a long record of strong opinions. It's to be expected that periodically these will come back to bite him. His usual tack is to deny that his old columns meant what their plain-word reading would indicate. For example, Krugman can't believe anybody thought [his] column (from 2002) should be construed as his endorsement of Greenspan trying to create a housing bubble.

When it comes to Social Security, here's what Krugman wrote in late 1996:

> Social Security is structured from the point of view of the recipients as if it were an ordinary retirement plan: what you get out depends on what you put in. So it does not look like a redistributionist scheme. In practice it has turned out to be strongly redistributionist, but only because of its Ponzi game aspect, in which each generation takes more out than it put in. Well, the Ponzi game will soon be over, thanks to changing demographics, so that the typical recipient hence-forth will get only about as much as he or she put in (and today's young may well get less than they put in).

As with his unfortunate housing-bubble article, here too Krugman has had to do damage control. After the above column floated around the Internet, Krugman tried to quell the giggling, claiming that anyone who tried to use him in support of Republican claims was playing "word games." Krugman then gave a link to [a] fascinating history of the original Ponzi scheme, courtesy of—the Social Security Administration! (It seems they must get this a lot.)

I was curious to see how the Social Security Administration would defend itself from the charge that it was a Ponzi scheme. Here's what they say:

> In contrast to a Ponzi scheme, dependent upon an unsustainable progression, a common financial arrangement is the so-called "pay-as-you-go" system. Some private pension systems, as well as Social Security, have used this design. A pay-as-you-go system can be visualized as a pipeline, with money from current contributors coming in the front end and money to current beneficiaries paid out the back end. . . .
>
> There is a superficial analogy between pyramid or Ponzi schemes and pay-as-you-go programs in that in both money

from later participants goes to pay the benefits of earlier participants. But that is where the similarity ends. . . .

As long as the amount of money coming in the front end of the pipe maintains a rough balance with the money paid out, the system can continue forever. There is no unsustainable progression driving the mechanism of a pay-as-you-go pension system and so it is not a pyramid or Ponzi scheme.

A Fair Charge

Contrary to the claims of Yglesias, Krugman, and the Social Security Administration, I don't think the "Ponzi scheme" charge is unfair in the slightest. When critics say Social Security is "unsustainable," they quite obviously mean that it can't keep up the current taxing and benefit schedules. Either taxes on workers will go up, promised benefits will be reduced, or some combination of the two. Krugman's 1996 column confirms that analysis, and the Social Security Administration's pipeline does too.

Up until now, retirees have been taking out more than they put in, and that can't continue—this pattern relied on finding ever more workers to join the system. In other words, it was a classic Ponzi scheme. I am not here to endorse candidate Rick Perry, but the point of his charge is obviously true: each generation can't keep taking more out of the system than it put in, once the demographics change.

The SSA's pipeline graphic is interesting. If *that* is ultimately what Social Security turns into, and if each generation of workers merely takes out "what it originally put in," then it means workers will earn a *zero-percent (real) return* on their "contributions" into the system.

Yes, that would certainly be "sustainable" in an accounting sense (at least with a stable age distribution in the population), but would it work politically? If politicians frankly told voters, "When we take $1,000 from you at age 25, don't worry, that $1,000 will be waiting for you when you're 65," would they be happy with this arrangement? Charles Ponzi too could have made his scheme more sustainable if he promised his investors a 0 percent rate of return, but then nobody would have been interested.

In fairness, Matt Yglesias points out that the pipeline method can yield a positive rate of return. If the workers at the left end of the pipe always pump in, say, 15 percent of their paycheck, then (if productivity grows over time as it normally does) 50 years later, when they are on the other end of the pipe, there will be more dollars shooting out. However, in this scenario we're back to an arrangement where each generation gets out more than it put in—what Krugman himself thought was a "Ponzi game aspect." In any event, Yglesias's framework is still vulnerable to demographic shifts.

Why Private-Sector Retirement Planning Works

The confusion in popular discussions of Social Security partly rests on the general ignorance of how an entire community can actually become richer through saving and investment. In other words, a lot of people believe (whether or not they've really thought it through carefully) that for every Sally out there who's saving $10,000 per year, there must be some Jim who's racking up $10,000 in debt. Therefore, whenever Sally starts living off her savings, people imagine that Jim must be cutting back on his own standard of living. At the communal level—so the thinking goes—everything is a wash, and we're just changing the distribution of "total output" based on which people were frugal and which were spendthrifts.

This mindset is totally wrong. I explain things methodically in chapter 10 of my introductory textbook [*Lessons for the Young Economist*], but here's the gist: It's possible for *everyone* in the entire community to "live below his means," that is, to consume less than his income and to save. The economy is then physically capable of reducing the output of consump-

What Is a Ponzi Scheme?

A Ponzi scheme is an investment fraud that involves the payment of purported returns to existing investors from funds contributed by new investors. Ponzi scheme organizers often solicit new investors by promising to invest funds in opportunities claimed to generate high returns with little or no risk. In many Ponzi schemes, the fraudsters focus on attracting new money to make promised payments to earlier-stage investors and to use for personal expenses, instead of engaging in any legitimate investment activity.

With little or no legitimate earnings, the schemes require a consistent flow of money from new investors to continue. Ponzi schemes tend to collapse when it becomes difficult to recruit new investors or when a large number of investors ask to cash out.

US Securities and Exchange Commission,
"Ponzi Schemes—Frequently Asked Questions,"
2012. www.sec.gov.

tion goods (TVs, sports cars, steak dinners, etc.) and increasing the output of investment or capital goods (drill presses, fertilizer, MRI machines, etc.). In the future, the larger quantities of various tools and equipment make the workers more productive than they otherwise would have been. That's why the standard of living can rise; the community is physically capable of cranking out more goods and services because of the past investments.

Think of it like this: During his working career, a farmer takes some of his crop every year and uses it to buy a component for a tractor. One year he buys a tire, another year he buys a steering wheel, and so on. After working for 45 years, the farmer is ready to retire. By this point, he has assembled a brand-new tractor. Now he no longer needs to use his labor to earn an income. Instead, he rents out use of the tractor to the younger workers (who otherwise would have to use their bare hands to till the soil, etc.).

From a certain viewpoint, the retired farmer would be "skimming off the top" every time he ate an ear of corn harvested after he no longer worked the fields himself. After all, that corn would be part of that year's harvest, so if the retired farmer ate it, there would be less corn available to the people who actually picked it. Yet the retired man's consumption wouldn't be financed through a "contribution" or "redistribution" from the young workers that year.

On the contrary, those young workers would be earning their full market wage (and if they were smart, they'd be saving some of it for their *own* retirement). The retired farmer would buy the corn on the open market, with the income he earned from renting out his tractor. There would be *more corn to go around* because he had spent decades assembling the tractor, and others in his cohort had built up stockpiles of fertilizer, hoes, irrigation equipment, etc.

Obviously my tale isn't realistic, but it serves to get across the essence of voluntary retirement planning. People can get out more than they put in (measured in physical terms) because of what Böhm-Bawerk called the superior physical productivity of roundabout processes. As I complained during the debates over George W. Bush's "privatization" proposals, many supposedly pro-market reformers want to get the magic of compound interest without the discipline of saving for decades.

A (Very Qualified) Defense of Charles Ponzi

Above I've explained why the "Ponzi scheme" accusation is accurate, in the context of modern political debates. However, there is a very important sense in which it is unfair—unfair to Charles Ponzi.

It's true that Ponzi engaged in fraud; his victims never would have "invested" with him, had he accurately explained the business model. Libertarians therefore agree with everybody else that Charles Ponzi was a criminal and would have to face legal consequences in any just legal order.

However, so far as we know Ponzi never *threatened* anybody. He didn't tell struggling young workers, "Give me 15 percent of your paycheck every week, so that I can make you a fantastic return—or else I'll send goons to kidnap you."

In this respect, Social Security isn't a Ponzi scheme after all. It's more analogous to mobsters shaking down people for protection money, because otherwise "bad things could happen."

No Choice

The complaints about Social Security are accurate: The only reason it has enjoyed such "success" thus far is that it relied on increasing contributions from each new generation of workers. Now that the demographics have turned against the system, it is literally unsustainable. We will see increased taxes on workers, reduced payments to beneficiaries, or some combination of the two.

In the voluntary private sector, people can plan for their own retirement through genuine saving and investment. They don't need to extract concessions from the next generation of workers, because the retirees' prior savings allow the creation of capital goods that will provide income when their bodies no longer can do so.

Finally, in one important respect a classic Ponzi scheme is *less* dangerous than Social Security: It relies on fooling people into voluntarily handing over their money. Once the fraud is detected, the danger is eliminated. In contrast, American workers have no choice but to "contribute" to Social Security, whether they like the deal or not.

> *"The suspicion stems in part from a mis-
> understanding about what Social Secu-
> rity is. It's not a retirement savings pro-
> gram; it's an insurance plan designed
> to help the elderly, the disabled and
> their families stay out of poverty."*

Social Security
Is Not a Ponzi Scheme

Los Angeles Times

The Los Angeles Times *is one of the premier daily newspapers
in the United States. In the following viewpoint, the editorial
staff points out that there are a lot of misconceptions about Social Security, many of which are being reinforced by the current
political climate. One of the most dangerous is that Social Security is a Ponzi scheme, an unsustainable government program
that will not exist by the time most young workers retire. In fact,
Social Security is an insurance plan—not a retirement plan—set
up as a pay-as-you-go system that can be tweaked by regular
adjustments to keep it viable for decades to come. Moreover, the
authors note, the US government has a vested interest in not defaulting on Social Security and making sure it remains an effective and popular program.*

As you read, consider the following questions:

1. According to the op-ed, what is Social Security considered to be?

2. When do the authors say that the last major set of changes in the payroll tax were made?

3. How much is the current valuation of the Social Security Trust Fund, according to the authors?

The conventional wisdom has long held that Social Security is the "third rail" of politics, so popular that criticizing it amounts to committing political suicide. Evidently no one bothered to warn Texas Gov. Rick Perry, who repeated his critique that Social Security is a "Ponzi scheme" shortly after entering the race for the Republican presidential nomination. His hyperbolic denunciation, which has resonated with segments of the GOP and the "tea party" movement, reflects some of the real problems in the 76-year-old program. But it misconstrues what those problems are and how they can be fixed.

Perry contends that it's a "monstrous lie" to tell young workers that Social Security is still going to be around when they retire. Never mind that Congress has periodically raised the payroll tax and adjusted the benefit formula to put the program back on solid ground. The fact that actuaries identify new threats to its long-term health seemingly every decade feeds the suspicion that there's something fundamentally wrong.

The suspicion stems in part from a misunderstanding about what Social Security is. It's not a retirement savings program; it's an insurance plan designed to help the elderly, the disabled and their families stay out of poverty. And unlike a savings program's returns, there isn't a direct relationship between what workers pay into Social Security and what they

How Did Ponzi Schemes Get Their Name?

The schemes are named after Charles Ponzi, who duped thousands of New England residents into investing in a postage stamp speculation scheme back in the 1920s. At a time when the annual interest rate for bank accounts was five percent, Ponzi promised investors that he could provide a 50% return in just 90 days. Ponzi initially bought a small number of international mail coupons in support of his scheme, but quickly switched to using incoming funds to pay off earlier investors.

US Securities and Exchange Commission,
"Ponzi Schemes—Frequently Asked Questions,"
2012. www.sec.gov.

get out of it. Instead, those who had high salaries receive a smaller percentage of their average wages than those who worked in low-paying jobs.

Pay-as-You-Go Systems

As with many insurance plans, Social Security is set up primarily as a pay-as-you-go system. Current workers' contributions are mainly used to fund current retirees' benefits. Here's the problem. The program was created in an era with high birthrates and a steady influx of new workers. As a result, there were far more workers contributing to the system than there were receiving benefits. That ratio of workers to retirees has declined over the years, increasing the cost pressure on younger workers. But other factors—such as shifting workforce patterns, wage growth and immigration—have reduced that pressure.

Congress responded to the demographic changes by increasing Social Security tax rates 20 times and the maximum amount of wages subject to the tax 43 times between 1937 and 2009, as well as gradually raising the age at which recipients could start collecting full retirement benefits. Benefits increased too, but there was no escaping the fact that later generations had to pay more for their Social Security benefits than their predecessors had.

The last major set of changes in the payroll tax, which were enacted in 1983, were designed to kill two birds with one stone. In addition to fixing a short-term shortfall, the increases were supposed to prepare for the retirement of the baby boom generation—an unusually large group whose numbers threatened to overwhelm the program. For about 20 years, the system would build up trillions of dollars in reserves by collecting more from workers than the program paid out in benefits. The reserves would then help pay for the boomers' benefits.

The System Needs Tweaking

Those changes were supposed to put the program on a sound financial footing for 75 years. By the mid-1990s, however, it became clear that Congress hadn't gone far enough. The latest projection is that the program will fall $6.5 trillion short over the coming 75 years. That's not because of the dwindling ratio of workers to retirees, however. An advisory panel reported in 1997 that lawmakers had correctly factored in that change. Instead, the main problems have been slower wage growth and larger disability benefit costs than anticipated, as well as the limitations of trying to measure a host of variables 75 years into the future.

In other words, Social Security isn't built on a faulty foundation. It does, however, need regular adjustments to keep the tax and benefit formulas in line. As the advisory panel noted in 1997, Congress needs to adjust it again—by broadening its tax base, increasing payroll taxes, raising the retirement age, reducing the annual increases in benefits or some combination thereof. The longer it waits to do so, the larger the adjustments will have to be.

Even if lawmakers do nothing, the Social Security program would soldier on indefinitely, albeit at a reduced level. The Social Security Trust Fund (currently valued at more than $2.6 trillion) would keep growing for about a decade, largely thanks to the interest it accumulates. Then it would help maintain the current rate of benefit growth until about 2036. Once the trust fund was exhausted, the benefits for retirees would fall sharply; payroll taxes would generate only enough money to pay 77% of the benefits owed under the current formula.

Even at that level, benefits should be at least as large for most retirees as the ones paid to retirees today. But such a sharp reduction would be unconscionable, considering how many Americans rely on Social Security just to get by. The program's monthly checks account for at least 90% of the income received by more than a third of today's 54 million beneficiaries.

Misconceptions About How the System Works

Perry contends that the day of reckoning for Social Security is coming far sooner than 2036. In his view, the trust fund is filled with worthless IOUs because Congress borrowed the money to cover part of the cost of operating the government. Those IOUs take the form of special Treasury securities that can't be sold to the public; instead, the Treasury Department has to buy them back. That means the federal government will have to borrow the money needed to redeem the trust fund's holdings unless it cuts spending or raises taxes enough to create a budget surplus. That borrowing won't require an increase in the debt limit, though—the "intragovernmental debt" owed to the trust fund is already included in the amount subject to the limit.

So no, the Social Security Trust Fund isn't stuffed with cash. But the securities in the trust fund are backed by the full faith and credit of the United States, just like T-bills or any other federal bond. Defaulting on them would cause an order-of-magnitude more damage to the U.S. credit rating, and in turn its economy, than Washington's recent brinkmanship over raising the debt ceiling. Such a step would be unthinkable, but then, so was a major presidential candidate calling Social Security a Ponzi scheme.

"The program is morally, philosophically, economically, and constitutionally indefensible. The whole system is built on misrepresentation, theft, and coercion."

Social Security Should Be Abolished

Laurence M. Vance

Laurence M. Vance is an author, blogger, columnist, and political advisor for The Future of Freedom Foundation, an educational foundation whose mission is to advance freedom by providing an uncompromising moral and economic case for individual liberty, free markets, private property, and limited government. In the following viewpoint, Vance states that Social Security should be abolished because it is an economically and morally indefensible program that fosters dependency and irresponsibility. It is fundamentally wrong to take money from working people and give it to someone else, Vance argues. He claims that the federal government has no authority to set up and maintain retirement, disability, survivor, or pension plans for nongovernment workers. Therefore, Vance concludes it should be eliminated and workers provide for their own retirements as they see fit.

As you read, consider the following questions:

1. According to the author, what were the recommendations of the President's Commission to Strengthen Social Security during the George W. Bush administration?

2. What percentage of the expenditures of Medicare Parts B and D are paid out of the federal government's general fund, as cited by Vance?

3. Does Vance believe that there is a contractual right to receive Social Security benefits?

Speaking at a conference for a finance trade association in Chicago, former President George W. Bush said that the biggest failure of his administration was not privatizing Social Security.

In 2001 the President's Commission to Strengthen Social Security was formed. This bipartisan, 16-member commission issued a report that included three reform proposals, all of which allowed workers to voluntarily transfer a portion of their Social Security taxes to a personal retirement account. At retirement, the workers' benefits would be offset by their personal account contributions. Bush called for reforming Social Security throughout his presidency. But although he had a Republican majority in Congress for more than four years of his presidency, no changes were made to the Social Security system.

The idea behind the privatization of Social Security is that workers should be able to have more control over their retirement savings by investing *some* of the money they would normally pay in Social Security taxes in a private retirement account.

The privatization idea was never very popular except among some conservatives and Beltway libertarians. And that's a good thing. Otherwise, we would have a new government bureaucracy to oversee the privatization and still be saddled

© Paul Fell / CartoonStock.com

with the massive Social Security bureaucracy. Privatization would entail billions in transition costs, accelerate the rate of insolvency of the current system, and yet provide no guaranteed return.

Saving Social Security

What has been realized about Social Security by people of all political persuasions is that as the birthrate continues its decline and fewer workers pay into the Social Security system, the "trust fund" will eventually be depleted as life expectancy increases and more retirees draw benefits. According to the 2010 annual reports of the Trustees of the Social Security and Medicare trust funds, "Social Security expenditures are expected to exceed tax receipts this year for the first time since 1983." Thus, now more than ever, will we hear—from Democrats and Republicans—about the need to fix, reform, strengthen, or save Social Security.

There have been a myriad of proposals offered to save Social Security. The method that has been used the most often since Social Security taxes were first levied in 1937 is an increase in the tax rate. The original rate was 2 percent (half paid by employees and half paid by employers). By 1960, the rate had tripled and continued to rise steadily. [President] Ronald Reagan is often praised as a great tax cutter, but it should be pointed out that the Social Security tax rate increased from 10.16 percent when he took office to 12.12 percent when he left. The rate has held steady at 12.4 percent since 1990.

Other proposals to save Social Security include raising the retirement age (currently 67 for those born in 1960 or later), means-testing of benefits, cutting benefits, raising taxes on benefits, delaying or eliminating the age of eligibility for reduced benefits, changing the assumptions used to calculate cost-of-living increases to benefits, reducing or eliminating cost-of-living increases, mandating the participation of certain workers who are not covered by Social Security, dedicating estate taxes to Social Security, raising or removing the wage base (currently $106,800), changing the assumptions used to set the initial benefit level (currently based on the 35 highest wage years), and investing the trust fund in something other than government bonds (as required by current law).

Another approach, of course, is simply to do nothing and make up the revenue shortfall from the federal government's general fund. About 75 percent of the expenditures of Medicare Parts B and D are already paid out of the general fund.

The Dishonesty of Social Security

Infinitely more important than the question of how to save Social Security is whether Social Security should be saved in the first place.

Although Social Security is presented as retirement insurance for which one pays premiums or contributions, it is not an insurance program, a savings account, a safety net, or an investment account. Social Security is an entitlement program, an income-transfer scheme, a wealth-redistribution plan. Money is simply taken from those who work and given to those who do not. The recipients maybe retired, disabled, or receiving survivors' benefits. They may not be able to work. They may have lost the family's provider. Social Security may be their only source of income. But none of that changes the nature of the system.

Social Security has been termed the third rail of politics. Any reform proposal that would in any way reduce benefits is political suicide. Social Security is the crown jewel of the welfare state. It is the largest entitlement program in the federal budget. Together with its cousin, Medicare, Social Security is responsible for more than a trillion dollars a year in income redistribution.

There is no real Social Security trust fund; there is no lock box; and there certainly isn't a retirement account with anyone's name on it. Payroll taxes collected are immediately spent to provide current Social Security payments. All taxes collected over benefits paid are "invested" in U.S. government securities on which interest is credited. The "trust fund" is just one gigantic IOU from the U.S. Treasury.

Social Security is also a gigantic Ponzi scheme that benefits those who get on board early. According to economist Walter Williams, a man reaching age 65 in the year 2000 could expect to receive $71,000 more in government transfer payments (of which the largest amount is Social Security) than he paid in taxes. But a 20-year-old man who entered the workforce in the year 2000 can expect to pay $312,000 more in taxes than he will ever receive in benefits.

There is no contractual right to receive Social Security benefits. Congress may amend and revise the Social Security benefit schedule at will. Social Security taxes exist simply for the purpose of raising revenue. On these points, see the cases *Helvering v. Davis* (1937) and *Fleming v. Nestor* (1960).

Social Security is so ingrained in American society that Republicans—even those who are viewed as staunch conservatives—defend Social Security as ardently as Democrats. Just look at the "Pledge to America" released by House Republicans a few weeks before the election last November [2012]:

> We will make the decisions that are necessary to protect our entitlement programs for today's seniors and future generations. That means requiring a full accounting of Social Security, Medicare, and Medicaid, setting benchmarks for these programs and reviewing them regularly, and preventing the expansion of unfunded liabilities.

Conservatives' protection of, accounting of, setting benchmarks for, and reviewing Social Security is a far cry from libertarian calls to repeal, eliminate, and abolish the program.

The libertarian view of Social Security is a no-brainer. The program is morally, philosophically, economically, and constitutionally indefensible. The whole system is built on misrepresentation, theft, and coercion. It shifts responsibility from the individual to society, from the family to the state, from the private to the public. The taking of someone's income for the purpose of giving it to someone else, whether the government takes it or a thief takes it, is immoral, no matter what the supposed good intentions of the taker may be.

Even if Social Security were an insurance program, even if it were optional, even if it were funded voluntarily, and even if it were solvent—the federal government has no authority and no business setting up and maintaining retirement, disability, survivor, or pension plans for non-government workers.

Social Security can be abolished. And it can be abolished today, once it is recognized for what it is: a relic from Roosevelt's New Deal that has fostered dependency and redistributed trillions of dollars.

> "Social Security has sufficient financing to pay benefits for decades to come. The challenge today is much different—it is to secure the program for the long-term future, usually defined as 75 years and perhaps beyond."

Social Security Should Be Strengthened

Janice Gregory

Janice Gregory is president of the National Academy of Social Insurance. In the following viewpoint, she observes that Social Security is a popular and effective program that Americans want to protect and strengthen for their generation and for those to come. Therefore, it is essential to come up with ways to improve the long-term financing of the program. Gregory suggests a number of options for consideration to raise revenues to close the shortfalls in Social Security. Such targeted improvements to the program would be affordable and fair, she contends, and would work to improve the American people's confidence in the program to stay viable and popular well into the future.

As you read, consider the following questions:

1. According to Gregory, what was the average annual Social Security benefit in 2010?

2. According to a 2009 poll by the National Academy of Social Insurance and the Rockefeller Foundation, what percentage of Americans agree it is critical to save Social Security for future generations?

3. According to a 2010 AARP survey, what percentage of adults oppose cutting Social Security to reduce the deficit?

Current policy discussions about the long-term financing of Social Security often hold up reforms enacted in 1983 as a model of balanced political compromise that might be replicated today. But a closer examination tells a different story with important ramifications for the current era.

1983 Crisis

First, unlike in 1983, today's Social Security program faces no near-term financial crisis. In 1983, the program's reserves dropped nearly to zero, and immediate action was required in order to pay all scheduled benefits on time; the challenge was to avert a short-term crisis. In 2010, Social Security has sufficient financing to pay benefits for decades to come. The challenge today is much different—it is to secure the program for the long-term future, usually defined as 75 years and perhaps beyond.

Second, in 1983 a bipartisan commission appointed by President Ronald Reagan and chaired by Alan Greenspan focused on the short-term crisis. It proposed a relatively balanced package of reforms designed to carry the program through the 1980s, the bulk of which Congress enacted. Some of these reforms also had an effect on the long-term finances of the program—but the commission's package failed to close the long-term gap that the program faced.

Congress closed that gap solely through an additional benefit reduction. It raised the retirement age from age 65 to 67 in the future, a benefit reduction still being phased in today. Congress did not add any new long-term revenue, even though providing future revenue to accommodate changing demographics had been a practice in the past.

Third, Social Security benefits already will be less adequate than in the past. Benefits as a percent of career average Social Security earnings are declining—from about 41 percent in 1986 to 39 percent in 2005 to an estimated 32 percent in 2030. Benefits are modest—about $14,000 annually on average in 2010—but are the main source of income for most of our elderly. And, as too many Americans are painfully aware, other sources of retirement income are becoming less secure and less adequate.

Despite growing economic uncertainty faced by working Americans, we will be spending less per Social Security beneficiary in the future. While the cost of the program will increase from about 5 percent of the economy today to about 6 percent 75 years from now, the percent of the population receiving benefits will increase from about 17 percent to about 25 percent.

Contrary to the primary focus of current discussions, the adequacy of benefits already is a growing concern that will become ever more compelling in the coming years. Adequacy must be a part of the current debate. Even low-cost, targeted changes can accomplish a great deal.

One change, for example, would help those who work long careers at low pay. A special minimum benefit was enacted in the 1970s for this population, but because it was not indexed to keep pace with wage growth as regular Social Security benefits are, it is no longer effective. The minimum benefit could be updated to 125 percent of the poverty line for someone who has worked 30 years and retires at the full-benefit age.

Revenue Increase

Paying for modest improvements like this and covering the projected long-term deficit facing Social Security would require additional financing equal to just over 2 percent of taxable payroll over 75 years. There are many options that could be considered to raise this revenue.

For example, in 1977, Congress set a goal of collecting FICA tax contributions on 90 percent of all covered wages. But because the earnings of those who make more than the cap on taxable income ($106,800 in 2010) have risen much faster in recent years than the earnings of others, only about 83 percent of earnings are subject to the FICA tax today. Gradually lifting the cap over a 10-year period to again cover 90 percent of earnings would eliminate about 39 percent of Social Security's projected long-term shortfall.

Another 13 percent could be eliminated by treating all employee contributions to salary-reduction plans, such as medical spending accounts and dependent care accounts, as 401(k) contributions are treated. The latter are exempt from income taxes but subject to FICA contributions for Social Security and Medicare.

Among other options, the remainder of the shortfall could be covered by potential FICA rate increases in the distant future, like those Congress has enacted throughout most of Social Security's history to keep the system in long-term balance. An increase could occur in 12 to 15 years when the program will start to draw down its trust fund reserves, and another in 40 or 60 years.

Strengthening Social Security

To some it may seem strange even to suggest a revenue increase. But Americans hold Social Security in a special category—one they are willing to support with their hard-earned money, as survey after survey reveals.

In 2009, for example, the National Academy of Social Insurance and the Rockefeller Foundation found that 77 percent of Americans—including 87 percent of Democrats, 75 percent of independents and 67 percent of Republicans—agree it is critical to preserve Social Security for future generations, even if it means increasing working Americans' contributions to the program. An AARP survey released in August 2010 found that 85 percent of adults oppose cutting Social Security to reduce the deficit, and 72 percent "strongly" oppose doing so.

Adopting targeted improvements to Social Security and a long-term financing plan to pay for future benefits would be equitable and affordable, and would reflect the views of the American people. Most importantly, it would give Americans greater confidence in their own economic future.

Periodical and Internet Sources Bibliography

The following articles have been selected to supplement the diverse views presented in this chapter.

Jared Bernstein — "A Reminder Why Protecting Social Security Is So Important," *On the Economy*, January 9, 2013.

Nita Ghei — "The Social Security Ponzi Scheme," *Washington Times*, August 10, 2012.

Tom Harkin — "A Real Proposal to Strengthen Social Security," *The Huffington Post*, December 7, 2012.

Ezra Klein — "Is Social Security a Ponzi Scheme?" *Washington Post*, October 11, 2011.

Andrew P. Napolitano — "Social Security *Is* a Ponzi Scheme," Fox News, April 26, 2012.

Brian Palmer — "What Would Happen If Social Security Disappeared?" *Slate*, September 8, 2011.

Richard M. Salsman — "Social Security Is Much Worse Than a Ponzi Scheme—and Here's How to End It," Forbes.com, September 27, 2011.

Jacob Sullum — "Is Social Security a Ponzi Scheme?," *Reason*, December 2011.

John Tamny — "The Ugly Truth About Social Security Is Revealed," Forbes.com, June 3, 2012.

USA Today — "Social Security Far from a 'Ponzi Scheme,'" September 11, 2011.

Christian E. Weller — "Building It Up, Not Tearing It Down," Center for American Progress, December 9, 2010.

OPPOSING
VIEWPOINTS®
SERIES

CHAPTER 4

What Medical Challenges Face an Aging Population?

Chapter Preface

The popularity of medical marijuana is growing in the United States. A November 2012 public opinion poll conducted by Reason-Rupe reported that 73 percent of Americans believed that medical marijuana should be legal with a doctor's prescription. Even a majority of seniors, a demographic generally not in favor of drug reform, favors making medical marijuana legal for those who need it. By 2013, eighteen states and Washington, DC, had legalized the use of medical marijuana. The trend toward medical marijuana legalization has been gaining momentum in the past decade, and holds promise for ailing seniors who can be helped from the medical benefits.

Marijuana has a long and turbulent history in the United States. During the Colonial period, farmers widely cultivated hemp from cannabis plants. During the 1700s subsidies were offered to settlers to encourage hemp cultivation and the manufacture of rope and canvas. It proved to be a useful and profitable crop for many American farmers.

The medicinal value of cannabis was publicized by an enterprising Irish physician, William O'Shaughnessy, who discovered the drug's therapeutic properties while working in India during the 1830s for the British East India Company. In his work there, he utilized marijuana resin to successfully treat rheumatism and relieve some symptoms of rabies, cholera, and tetanus. After he returned to England in 1841, he introduced the drug to Western medicine. It did not take long for other physicians to experiment with marijuana resin to treat a range of conditions, including incontinence, venereal disease, and skin rashes.

By the beginning of the twentieth century, however, the popularity of marijuana for medicinal use had peaked. The drug had also become associated with crime, drug addiction, and moral debauchery after the media began to report its popularity with musicians, artists, and people in show business. The US Federal Bureau of Narcotics painted marijuana as a dangerous and addictive drug that would lure young people into addiction, poverty, and moral dissipation. By 1937, 23 states had outlawed marijuana. That same year, the US government passed the Marihuana Tax Act, which made it illegal to use marijuana except for medical purposes.

The Controlled Substances Act of 1970 banned the use of medical marijuana, declaring that the drug had no proven and accepted medicinal use. Marijuana was classified as a Schedule I drug, along with addictive and dangerous substances such as heroin and LSD. Today, marijuana is still categorized as a Schedule I drug, despite the attempts of medical researchers and scientists to change its official classification. These medical professionals argue that marijuana can successfully help conditions like chronic pain and nausea, anxiety, post-traumatic stress disorder, and glaucoma. Marijuana does have proven medical uses, they maintain, and should be used to bring relief to patients who need it.

Improving access to medical marijuana for seniors is one of the subjects discussed in the following chapter, which explores some of the medical issues relevant to an aging population. Other viewpoints in the chapter examine the need for long-term care for seniors, the epidemic of Alzheimer's and dementia in the elderly, and rising rates of sexually transmitted disease, depression, and substance abuse among older Americans.

"While the aging of America's population has been foreseen for decades, little
has been done to prepare the health
and long-term-care workforce for its
arrival."

Caring for an Aging America in the Twenty-First Century

Robyn I. Stone and Linda Barbarotta

Robyn I. Stone is the executive director of LeadingAge Center for Applied Research, and Linda Barbarotta is a consultant. In the following viewpoint, they suggest that America's aging popula-tion will require a highly trained, competent workforce in a vari-ety of settings in order to provide high-quality, long-term health care. Stone and Barbarotta outline several factors that make building such a committed workforce challenging, including the lack of value society places on geriatric services, a lack of geriat-ric education and training, and inadequate investment in educa-tion and training. The recent passage of the Patient Protection and Affordable Care Act is promising because it contains provi-sions that support geriatric education and financial incentives to encourage qualified people to enter professions that provide geri-atric care, they report.

Robyn I. Stone and Linda Barbarotta, "Caring for an Aging America in the Twenty-First Century," *Generations*, Winter 2010–2011. Copyright © 2011 by the American Society on Aging. All rights reserved. Reproduced by permission.

As you read, consider the following questions:

1. According to the authors, how many additional health care workers will the United States need just to maintain the current ratio of health care workers to the population by 2030?

2. What percentage of high school students interested in nursing do the authors report have no interest in specializing in geriatrics?

3. When was the Committee on the Future HealthCare Workforce for Older Americans convened, according to Stone and Barbarotta?

In January 2011, the first baby boomers turned age 65. Over the next twenty years, the number of adults who are ages 65 and older will double. The population of those ages 85 and older—the group most likely to need acute, primary, and long-term care—is expected to increase five-fold. One in five Americans will be of age 65 or older, compared with 12 percent today (Institute of Medicine, 2008).

While this demographic phenomenon is to be celebrated, it is also expected to place increasing demands on those who care for our elderly population—a group that uses considerably more services than younger people and whose health and long-term-care needs are often more complex. Elders are more likely to suffer from multiple chronic physical and mental illnesses, have higher levels of functional disability, use multiple medications, and have higher rates of dementia and other cognitive impairments (Medicare Payment Advisory Commission, 2007).

These demands require an educated, highly trained, competent workforce across all settings where people receive care—the hospital, a physician's office or clinic, a nursing home, assisted living (or other residential care setting), and private homes and apartments. The workforce ranges from the direct-care workers who provide hands-on care to a financially, racially, and ethnically diverse population, to the variety of clinicians who address the complex health and long-term-care needs of this population, to the managers and administrators who oversee the systems that deliver care.

This special issue of *Generations* recognizes the demographic reality that will be driving much of the health and long-term-care demand over the next twenty years and the need to develop a quality workforce to care for an aging America in the short and long term. The purpose of this special issue is to review the state of the art in the development of this workforce; to highlight the various policy and practice issues across professions and settings that are impeding or enhancing the development of this workforce; and to heighten awareness about the critical nature of these issues among the various stakeholders (policy makers, regulators, providers, professional organizations, educators, consumers, and families) who stand to benefit from the development of a quality eldercare workforce.

Why Workforce Matters

The development of a competent, committed workforce to care for our aging society is important and timely for two primary reasons. First, the supply of health and long-term-care workers does not currently meet demand and will certainly fall short of the increased demands expected in the future (Mather, 2007). Second, even if the numbers of workers were there, that is not sufficient: it is not possible to develop a quality and cost-effective delivery system without a well-trained, competent workforce that understands how to deliver care to older adults.

Concerns About Supply

It has been estimated that the United States will need an additional 3.5 million healthcare workers by 2030 just to maintain the current ratio of healthcare workers to the population

(Mather, 2007). And while the general need for professionals who care for older adults is high, the particular need for geriatric specialists is even greater. This trend is consistent across all professions including physicians (Association of Directors of Geriatric Academic Programs, 2007), nurses (Kovner, Mezey, and Harrington, 2002), social workers (Center for Health Workforce Studies, 2006), and other occupational categories. The current and projected lack of professionals and direct-care workers is particularly dramatic in the long-term-care sector (Harahan and Stone, 2009). The needed distribution of the health and long-term-care workforce for older Americans varies by state and the individual profession (Institute of Medicine, 2008). The recruitment and retention of healthcare professionals in rural areas are particularly challenging (Institute of Medicine, 2005). This is important to consider when assessing the healthcare needs of the geriatric population, since older adults are disproportionately overrepresented in rural communities (Hawes et al., 2005).

While the lack of supply is a challenge, it also provides an economic opportunity for many communities. Over the next twenty years, much of the job growth will be in the health and long-term-care sectors. Investments in a quality eldercare workforce, therefore, will be an important economic driver in the coming years.

The Workforce and Quality

Although it is intuitively obvious that a quality health and long-term-care system cannot exist without a quality workforce to provide the care and manage the system, this relationship has, for the most part, been taken for granted. Several of the articles in this special issue of *Generations* underscore the fact that a knowledgeable, competent workforce—well-trained in geriatrics and gerontological principles and practices—is essential to achieving better quality of care and quality of life

© Grizelda / CartoonStock.com

outcomes for elderly consumers of health and long-term care (see Bragg and Chin Hansen, page 11; Harahan, page 20; Seavey, page 27).

The interdisciplinary team approach to service delivery—the core of geriatric practice—has been linked to better quality across a range of settings (Coleman and Berenson, 2004). The literature emphasizes the critical role that well-prepared licensed nurses play—particularly in nursing home settings—in improving the quality of care (Harrington et al., 2002; Rantz, 2003; Bostick et al., 2006). Several studies have shown that geriatric nurse practitioners can have a positive effect on nursing home residents' care outcomes (Garrard et al., 1990; Rosenfelt et al., 2004). Another study found a positive relationship between having a certified medical director trained specifically in the medical director's role (based on geriatric principles and best practices) and nursing home quality outcomes (Rowland et al., 2009). Analyzing nursing home deficiency data from the Centers for Medicare and Medicaid Online Survey Certification and Reporting database, the research team found that the standardized quality score of facilities with certified medical directors were higher than the scores of facilities lacking a medical director with a special certification.

Challenges to Developing a Quality Health and Long-Term-Care Workforce

A number of factors challenge the successful development of this workforce. These include the lack of value ascribed to the aging services field and the occupations within the field; the lack of recognition of the importance of geriatric and gerontological education and training; and the consequent lack of appropriate investments in education and training that are knowledge- and competency-based across the full spectrum of professions.

Lack of Value

Aging services occupations are undervalued in the United States. Ageism in the broader culture, the sensationalizing of nursing home and assisted living problems in the media, and negative attitudes of educators and leaders in professional schools and associations conspire to reinforce the image of "caring for the elderly" as a poor career choice (Kaiser Family Foundation, 2007). Among high school students considering a nursing career, for example, almost half have no interest in specializing in geriatrics, whereas 87 percent report having an interest in pediatric nursing (Evercare, 2007).

This undervalued status translates into noncompetitive compensation and benefits for all staff categories in the clinical and managerial arenas. Within the field there exists a hierarchy in which individuals working in hospitals receive higher compensation and better benefits than those working in nursing home care or homecare. Compared with registered nurses who work in hospital settings, registered nurses working in nursing homes or other extended-care facilities receive lower annual earnings on average, even though they work more hours per week, incur more hours of overtime, and have a larger percentage of overtime hours that are mandatory (Bureau of Health Professions, 2006). In 2007, *Forbes Magazine* profiled personal and home care aide jobs as one of the top twenty-five worst-paying occupations in America (Maidment, 2007). Stakeholders in some states have observed that acute-care hospitals are able to draw staff away from long-term-care employers by offering higher salaries and better benefits (Center for Health Workforce Studies, 2006). As well, aging services providers have a diminished capacity to increase wages because more than 70 percent of their financing comes from Medicaid and Medicare, which seek to limit costs regardless of labor market conditions.

The convergence of these issues creates significant recruitment challenges for educational institutions that are attempting to develop geriatric and gerontological programs, and for providers who are looking to hire individuals with the appropriate knowledge and competencies. These barriers also negatively affect the pipeline for a future workforce that will be needed to meet increasing demand.

Unrecognized Lack of Geriatric Education and Training

A number of the articles in this issue of *Generations* highlight the fact that the importance of geriatric and gerontological education and training is not widely recognized by most individuals and groups that have a stake in the current and future status of our health and long-term-care system. These include the majority of policy makers, regulators, providers, educators, and consumers. Even those who believe in the new models of care that are described by Katz and Frank (page 82) and Reinhard (page 75) in this issue, assume that if financial and regulatory incentives are aligned, the development and implementation of person-centered, integrated, coordinated care programs will magically occur. Unfortunately, the lack of attention to and wide-scale adoption of geriatric and gerontological principles and best practices could translate into program failure and the squandering of precious resources.

Inadequate Investment in Education and Training

The undervalued nature of the field and the lack of recognition of the importance of geriatrics and gerontology undermine the development and sustainability of a quality health and long-term-care workforce for our aging society. The preparation of potential candidates for administrative and clinical positions is out of sync with the realities of current and future demand. As noted in several articles within this issue, medical, nursing, and social work students have little exposure to geriatrics and gerontology in their curricula or clinical placements. Administrators, nurses, and medical directors are poorly prepared for the management and supervisory roles with which they are charged, and there are few in-service training programs to help those who are already employed in these positions (Bowers, Esmond, and Jacobson, 2003; Institute of Medicine, 2008; Resnick et al., 2009).

The strategies employed by regulators and educators to prepare and license or certify the workforce, and to assure that personnel are able to keep pace with changes in the clinical knowledge base and new technologies, are not effective. There are developing competency-based standards that would help guide the workforce across occupations and settings, but these standards have not been widely disseminated or adopted at the policy and practice levels. Additionally, there is a huge shortfall of personnel who are competent and committed to educating and preparing both professional and direct-care workers for careers in delivering services to older adults. This translates into a dearth of people—of those who are currently working and of those who are in the pipeline—that are adequately trained and educated to assume increasingly complex jobs across the continuum of services.

Opportunities for Policy and Practice Change

While the aging of America's population has been foreseen for decades, little has been done to prepare the health and long-term-care workforce for its arrival (Institute of Medicine, 2008: 3). A number of efforts over the past few years, however, have helped to raise this issue to a priority level in both the policy and practice arenas. In 2008, the Institute of Medicine (IOM) created a Committee on the Future Health Care Workforce for Older Americans to assess the projected future healthcare status and health-care services utilization of older Americans; explore the best use of the healthcare workforce to meet the needs of the elderly population, including the most promising models to ensure high-quality, cost-effective service delivery, as well as the roles and types of providers required to successfully implement these models; determine the types of education and training needed to deliver services to elders, and the financial and other incentives that will best facilitate recruitment and retention; and recommend policy solutions to these challenges (Institute of Medicine, 2008: 3).

The report prepared by this committee, *Retooling for an Aging America*, was a seminal work that identified the key challenges, laid out a blueprint for action, and stimulated energy, excitement, and interest in policy and practice circles. With support from a number of foundations committed to developing a quality health and long-term-care workforce for older adults, a national coalition of professional, provider, and consumer organizations created the Eldercare Workforce Alliance (EWA) to spearhead implementation of the IOM's recommendations. The Alliance was instrumental in getting a number of workforce provisions into healthcare reform—the Patient Protection and Affordable Care Act (ACA)—that support geriatric education and financial incentives to encourage people to enter professional fields related to caring for the elderly population. The EWA is currently focused on ensuring that these provisions are adequately funded and successfully implemented as well as continuing to raise awareness about the need for this workforce among policy makers at the federal and state levels.

The ACA provisions related to the development of new payment incentives and delivery models to better serve Medicare beneficiaries and "dual eligible" (individuals covered by both Medicare and Medicaid) have also spotlighted the need for a knowledgeable, skilled eldercare workforce to actually achieve the ACA goals "on the ground." But successful development and implementation of the various integrated and coordinated care models, transitional care programs, and bundled payment methodologies that hold organizations accountable for quality care and costs will not occur magically—even if the financial incentives are perfectly aligned. They will depend, in large part, on the existence of professional staff across the full range of occupations and settings that understands how to coordinate person-centered services and integrate care through geriatric-based, holistic approaches that use interdisciplinary teams and that consider the most efficient ways of achieving quality outcomes.

Conclusion

The development of a quality eldercare workforce is no longer a backwater issue. The IOM report and the ACA provisions have established an important foundation upon which to build a workforce development agenda and to achieve actionable results. The development of a quality workforce to care for an aging America will require solutions at the policy, education, and practice levels. This issue of *Generations* underscores both the challenges and the opportunities that our nation faces over the next thirty years, and presents expert analysis, research findings, and unique insights that will, hopefully, form a roadmap to success.

| "*Dementia is overwhelming not only for the people who have it, but also for their caregivers and families.*"

Dementia: A Public Health Priority: Executive Summary

World Health Organization

The World Health Organization (WHO) is the United Nations agency devoted to monitoring and improving global health. In the following viewpoint, the rising global rate of dementia and its implications are examined in detail. According to WHO, in many countries, there is a lack of awareness and understanding of dementia, which results in stigmatization and barriers to effective diagnosis and care. To overcome these barriers, dementia should be considered a top priority on the public health agenda in every country around the world, WHO suggests. Strategies to address dementia should include advocacy, strengthening existing health systems, supporting caregivers and research, and developing effective new policies and plans.

As you read, consider the following questions:

1. According to the World Health Organization (WHO), what was the total number of people with dementia worldwide in 2010?

2. What does WHO estimate as the total worldwide cost of dementia in 2010?

3. Why does the report identify capacity-building of the workforce to be essential when dealing with dementia?

The world's population is ageing. Improvements in health care in the past century have contributed to people living longer and healthier lives. However, this has also resulted in an increase in the number of people with noncommunicable diseases, including dementia. Although dementia mainly affects older people, it is not a normal part of ageing. Dementia is a syndrome, usually of a chronic or progressive nature, caused by a variety of brain illnesses that affect memory, thinking, behaviour and ability to perform everyday activities.

Dementia is overwhelming not only for the people who have it, but also for their caregivers and families. It is one of the major causes of disability and dependency among older people worldwide. There is lack of awareness and understanding of dementia, at some level, in most countries, resulting in stigmatization, barriers to diagnosis and care, and impacting caregivers, families and societies physically, psychologically and economically. Dementia can no longer be neglected but should be considered a part of the public health agenda in all countries.

The objective of this report is to raise awareness of dementia as a public health priority, to articulate a public health approach and to advocate for action at international and national levels based on the principles of inclusion, integration, equity and evidence.

Burden of Dementia

We have a growing body of evidence on the global prevalence and incidence of dementia, the associated mortality and the global economic cost. Most of the information is from high-income countries with some data becoming increasingly available from low- and middle-income countries (LMIC).

Prevalence and incidence projections indicate that the number of people with dementia will continue to grow, particularly among the oldest old, and countries in demographic transition will experience the greatest growth. The total number of people with dementia worldwide in 2010 is estimated at 35.6 million and is projected to nearly double every 20 years, to 65.7 million in 2030 and 115.4 million in 2050. The total number of new cases of dementia each year worldwide is nearly 7.7 million, implying one new case every four seconds.

The total estimated worldwide costs of dementia were US$ 604 billion in 2010. In high-income countries, informal care (45%) and formal social care (40%) account for the majority of costs, while the proportionate contribution of direct medical costs (15%) is much lower. In low-income and lower-middle-income countries direct social care costs are small, and informal care costs (i.e. unpaid care provided by the family) predominate. Changing population demographics in many LMIC may lead to a decline in the ready availability of extended family members in the coming decades.

Research identifying modifiable risk factors of dementia is in its infancy. In the meantime, primary prevention should focus on targets suggested by current evidence. These include countering risk factors for vascular disease, including diabetes, midlife hypertension, midlife obesity, smoking, and physical inactivity.

Country Preparedness for Dementia

The challenges to governments to respond to the growing numbers of people with dementia are substantial. A broad public health approach is needed to improve the care and quality of life of people with dementia and family caregivers. The aims and objectives of the approach should either be articulated in a stand-alone dementia policy or plan or be inte-

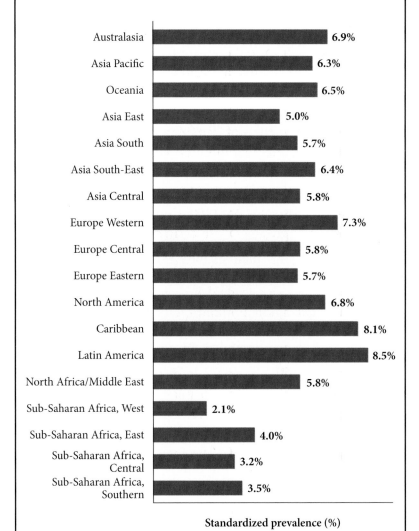

Estimated Prevalence of Dementia for Persons Aged 60 and Over

Region	Prevalence
Australasia	6.9%
Asia Pacific	6.3%
Oceania	6.5%
Asia East	5.0%
Asia South	5.7%
Asia South-East	6.4%
Asia Central	5.8%
Europe Western	7.3%
Europe Central	5.8%
Europe Eastern	5.7%
North America	6.8%
Caribbean	8.1%
Latin America	8.5%
North Africa/Middle East	5.8%
Sub-Saharan Africa, West	2.1%
Sub-Saharan Africa, East	4.0%
Sub-Saharan Africa, Central	3.2%
Sub-Saharan Africa, Southern	3.5%

Standardized prevalence (%)

Note: Standardized to Western Europe population, by Global Burden of Disease region.

TAKEN FROM: World Health Organization, "Dementia: A Public Health Priority," 2012. www.who.int.

grated into existing health, mental health or old-age policies and plans. Some high-income countries have launched policies, plans, strategies or frameworks to respond to the impact of dementia.

There are several key issues that are common to many national dementia policies and plans, and these may be necessary to ensure that needs are addressed in an effective and sustainable manner. These include: scoping the problem; involving all the relevant stakeholders, including civil society groups; identifying priority areas for action; implementing the policy and plan; committing resources; having intersectoral collaboration; developing a time frame; and monitoring and evaluation.

The priority areas of action that need to be addressed within the policy and plan include raising awareness, timely diagnosis, commitment to good quality continuing care and services, caregiver support, workforce training, prevention and research.

People with dementia and their families face significant financial impact from the cost of providing health and social care and from reduction or loss of income. Universal social support through pensions and insurance schemes could provide protection to this vulnerable group.

Formal recognition of the rights of people with dementia and their caregivers through legislation and regulatory processes will help reduce discriminatory practices. Fundamental to upholding a person's rights is the recognition of capacity in persons with dementia. Where capacity is impaired due to dementia, legal provisions should recognize and protect the right to appropriate autonomy and self-determination including substitute or supported decision-making and procedures for implementing advance directives. Education and support relating to ethical decision-making and human rights should be an essential part of capacity-building for all involved in providing dementia care, including policy-makers, professionals and families.

Health and Social Systems Development

The health and social care needs of the large and rapidly growing numbers of frail dependent older persons should be a matter of great concern for policy-makers in all countries. This is particularly so for LMIC which will experience the greatest increase in ageing in the coming decades.

This challenges governments to develop and improve services for people with dementia, focusing on earlier diagnosis, provision of support in the community, and a responsive health and social care sector. Integrated and coordinated health and social pathways and services will be needed to cater for the changing needs of people with dementia and their caregivers. Such pathways should ensure that the needs of specific or minority population groups are taken into account.

Improved community support will assist families to provide care for longer and to delay or reduce reliance on high-cost residential care. Where resources are finite, especially in LMIC, a focus on community outreach could be an efficient use of scarce resources to improve the quality of life of people with dementia and their caregivers. The effectiveness of task shifting (with appropriate guidelines and training) in LMIC should be further evaluated as a solution to the under-supply of a professional workforce.

Capacity-building of the workforce is essential to improve knowledge and awareness of the benefits of a coordinated response to care. Dementia care, long-term care and chronic disease management incorporating a multidisciplinary team should form part of professional education and should be supported by the development of appropriate practice guidelines. In a world with an increasingly mobile population, the migrant workforce brings its own set of challenges that need to be understood and addressed.

Support for Informal Care and Caregivers

Dementia has an immense impact on the lives of the family, and particularly the person who takes the primary role in providing care. Most care is provided by family and other informal support systems in the community and most caregivers are women. However, changing population demographics may reduce the availability of informal caregivers in the future.

The provision of care to a person with dementia can result in significant strain for those who provide most of that care. The stressors are physical, emotional and economic. A range of programmes and services have been developed in high-income countries to assist family caregivers and to reduce strain. The beneficial effects of caregiver interventions in decreasing the institutionalization of the care recipient have been clearly demonstrated.

Evidence from LMIC also suggests that home-based support for caregivers of persons with dementia, emphasizing the use of locally-available low-cost human resources, is feasible, acceptable and leads to significant improvements in caregiver mental health and in the burden of caring. Despite evidence of effectiveness, there have been no successful examples of scale-up in any of the health systems in which the evaluative research has been conducted. Further research should focus on implementation in order to inform the process of scale-up.

Despite the availability of services in some countries or parts of countries, there are barriers to uptake. Lack of awareness of services, lack of understanding or stigma attached to the syndrome, previous poor experience with services, and cultural, language and financial barriers creates obstacles to service utilization. Information and education campaigns for the public—including people with dementia, their caregivers and families—can improve service utilization by raising awareness, improving understanding and decreasing stigmatizing attitudes.

Support is needed to enable informal caregivers to be able to continue in their role for as long as possible. Support includes information to aid understanding, skills to assist in caring, respite to enable engagement in other activities, and financial support.

Awareness-Raising and Advocacy

Despite the growing impact globally, a lack of understanding of dementia contributes to fears and to stigmatization. For those who are living with dementia (both the person and their family), the stigma contributes to social isolation and to delays in seeking diagnosis and help.

There is an urgent need to improve the awareness and understanding of dementia across all levels of society as a step towards improving the quality of life of people with dementia and their caregivers. Governments have a role to play in resourcing public awareness campaigns and in ensuring that key stakeholders are involved in such campaigns.

Awareness-raising campaigns should be relevant to the context and audience. They should be accurate, effective and informative and should be developed in consultation with people with dementia, their families and other stakeholders, including civil society.

The Way Forward

The findings of this report demonstrate that dementia is a global public health challenge. A range of actions is required to improve care and services for people with dementia and their caregivers. These actions include advocacy and awareness-raising, developing and implementing dementia policies and plans, health system strengthening, capacity-building, supporting caregivers and research. The actions need to be context-specific and culturally relevant.

> *"The factors driving the rise of STDs in the older set include Americans living longer, healthier lives and a new class of medications, which include Viagra, that's making more sex possible."*

Seniors' Sex Lives Are Up—And So Are STD Rates

Marni Jameson

Marni Jameson is a reporter for the Orlando Sentinel. *In the following viewpoint, she investigates the rising rates of sexually transmitted diseases (STDs) among the aging. Health care authorities suggest that because today's seniors are living longer, healthier, and more active lives than earlier generations, they are staying sexually active longer. Sex-enhancing pharmaceuticals are also a factor in levels of sexual activity among seniors. However, there seems to be a lack of safe-sex education in older generations, which leads to higher transmission rates of STDs. To respond to the troubling trend, Medicare is considering providing STD screenings and behavioral counseling for seniors.*

As you read, consider the following questions:

1. According to the Centers for Disease Control, as reported by Jameson, how much did the number of reported cases of syphilis and chlamydia rise among those 55 and older between 2005 and 2009?

2. According to an Indiana University study cited by the author, what age group used condoms the least?

3. In a 2007 *New England Journal of Medicine* study referred to by Jameson, what percent of women aged 65 to 74 reported having had sex in the previous year?

Across the nation, and especially in the Sunshine State, the free-love generation is continuing to enjoy an active—if not always healthy—sex life.

At a stage in life when many would expect sexually transmitted diseases to be waning, seniors are noticeably ahead of the national curve.

In the five years from 2005 to 2009, the number of reported cases of syphilis and chlamydia among those 55 and older increased 43 percent, according to the Centers for Disease Control.

In Central Florida, the rise is even more dramatic. Among those 55 and older, the reported cases of syphilis and chlamydia increased 71 percent in that same five-year period. That puts Central Florida ahead of the state, which saw a 62 percent rise in those two sexually transmitted infections among the same age group.

The rates at which syphilis and chlamydia increased among older adults outpaced the nation's average. Among all age groups nationwide, reported cases of syphilis increased 60 percent between 2005 and 2009; among those in the 55 to 64 age group, it went up 70 percent. Meanwhile, the incidence of chlamydia rose 27 percent among all ages, and double that among the older group.

As a result of the national trend among seniors, Medicare is considering providing coverage for STD screenings for seniors. Last month, the Centers for Medicare and Medicaid office announced that it was looking into adding STD exams to the national health insurance program, which already pays for HIV screenings. Medicare also is weighing the benefits of paying for behavioral counseling for sexually active seniors.

The factors driving the rise of STDs in the older set include Americans living longer, healthier lives and a new class of medications, which include Viagra, that's making more sex possible. Many older adults didn't get the safe-sex messages that younger generations received, say experts, so their condom use is lower. In addition, more seniors are living in group retirement communities where there's more socializing.

"These seniors may lose a spouse, then get lonely," said Dr. Jason Salagubang, a geriatrician on staff at Florida Hospital Apopka. "They're living in retirement communities with others in the same boat, and sparks fly."

Julia Gill, director of the division of disease control for the Florida Department of Health, says the heavy marketing for sex-enhancing pharmaceuticals aimed at seniors and Florida's lure as a retirement destination are likely causing the state's seniors—particularly those in Central Florida—to lead the trend.

"Certainly we've noted the change and will adjust our outreach, testing and marketing efforts to reflect that," Gill said.

Besides Viagra, other medications such as hormone replacements are helping seniors remain sexually active longer. Progesterone and estrogen creams help make sex more comfortable for women, while testosterone replacement drugs give libido a boost in both men and women.

Finally, a more open sexual attitude has contributed to the rising infection rate. "The flower children who were in their

The Facts About Syphilis

- Syphilis (SI fi lis) is a sexually transmitted disease (STD).

- Anyone can get syphilis.

- Many people who have syphilis don't know it. You can have syphilis even if you don't notice any symptoms.

- The first symptom is a painless, round, and red sore that can appear anywhere you've had sex.

- You can pass syphilis to others without knowing it.

- Washing the genitals, urinating, or douching after sex will not prevent syphilis.

- Syphilis is easy to treat and cure.

- If you do not treat syphilis, it can lead to serious health problems.

Centers for Disease Control and Prevention,
"Syphilis: The Facts," 2012.

20s back in the 1960s are now in their 70s," said Salagubang. "They're the make-love-not-war generation, and old habits die hard."

Just because seniors are older and wiser, doesn't mean they're not susceptible to the same diseases as everyone else, Salagubang said. In fact, they're more susceptible.

As people age, their immune systems tend to weaken, and other health problems make them more prone to infection. Medications for heart disease, hypertension and diabetes also cause seniors to be more likely to pick up what's going around.

Because STDs often have no symptoms, they frequently go untreated and make seniors more prone to other infections, said Salagubang. And these infections will make other conditions, such as diabetes or heart disease, worse.

"If I think a patient may be sexually active, I suggest he or she gets screened," said Salagubang. "I let patients know that STDs and HIV are on the rise among seniors, and are a lot more common than many seniors think."

Although older Americans account for a relatively small proportion of new STD diagnoses overall, providing them education and services to help protect them from infection is critical, said Rachel Powell, CDC spokeswoman.

"Many older Americans face unique prevention challenges, including discomfort in discussing sexual behaviors with physicians and partners, and discomfort discussing condom use," she said.

Given the changing sexual climate for seniors, Dr. Connie Micklavzina, a gynecologist at Winnie Palmer Hospital in Orlando has started asking her older patients more questions, including whether they would like to be screened for sexually transmitted diseases.

"Often I see a huge look of relief on their faces, because they are too embarrassed to ask," said Micklavzina, who's been in practice 25 years. "The responsibility of bringing this up should be on the practitioner, not the patient, to make the conversation easier."

Practitioners should not make any assumptions based on a patient's age, or social or marital status, Micklavzina added. "It has nothing to do with it."

She also broaches the subject of condom use. "I'm surprised by the number of women in their 50s and 60s who aren't insisting that their partners use condoms."

A study conducted by sex researchers at Indiana University found that in the United States, condom use was lowest among men over age 50. Men in their 50s reported using a condom only 28 percent of the time with a casual partner. By comparison, men in the 18 to 39 age-range used a condom with casual partners at least 50 percent of the time.

"We often assume that younger people are at greater risk for sexual health challenges like HIV and STD," said Michael Reece, director of the Center for Sexual Health Promotion, at Indiana University. "However, these data suggest that younger Americans are using condoms more consistently than older Americans."

The fact that older Americans aren't worried about preventing pregnancy accounts for some of the lower condom use, but this age group clearly needs more education about the risks of unsafe sex, Reece said.

According to a 2007 study reported in the *New England Journal of Medicine*, 67 percent of men and 39 percent of women aged 65 to 74 surveyed reported having had sex in the previous year; 38 percent of men aged 75 to 85 reported the same.

"We should not be profiling people based on their age, and making assumptions about their sexual activity," said Dr. Stacey Landau, ob-gyn at the University of Chicago and author of the study. "Removing age-based profiling with respect to STD screenings is a good idea."

| "For the elderly population, depression can come in different sizes and shapes."

Depression in Older Persons

Ken Duckworth, M.D., NAMI Medical Director

The National Alliance on Mental Illness (NAMI) is a US mental health organization. In the following viewpoint, the problem of depression in the aging is examined. Depression in older Americans is common and often goes undiagnosed and untreated, with doctors and family mistaking the symptoms as signs of grieving, dementia, Alzheimer's disease, or other conditions. This has grave consequences, NAMI warms, as untreated depression can lead to cognitive decline, mental illness, and even suicide. It is important to recognize the signs of depression in order to get treatment. NAMI reports that medication, psychotherapy, and other treatment methods have proven to be effective treatments for depression in aging men and women.

As you read, consider the following questions:

1. According to the National Alliance on Mental Illness (NAMI), how many Americans aged 65 or older suffer from depression?

2. Why are older women at greater risk for depression, according to NAMI?

3. According to Duckworth, what percentage of clinically depressed individuals can be effectively treated by medication, psychotherapy, or electroconvulsive therapy?

Depression affects more than 6.5 million of the 35 million Americans aged 65 or older. Most people in this stage of life with depression have been experiencing episodes of the illness during much of their lives. Others may experience a first onset in late life—even in their 80s and 90s. Depression in older persons is closely associated with dependency and disability and causes great distress for the individual and the family.

Why does depression in the older population often go untreated?

Depression in elderly people often goes untreated because many people think that depression is a normal part of aging—a natural reaction to chronic illness, loss and social transition. Elderly people do face noteworthy challenges to their connections through loss, and also face medical vulnerability and mortality. For the elderly population, depression can come in different sizes and shapes. Many elderly people and their families don't recognize the symptoms of depression, aren't aware that it is a medical illness and don't know how it is treated. Others may mistake the symptoms of depression as signs of:

- dementia

- Alzheimer's disease

- arthritis

- cancer

- heart disease

- Parkinson's disease

- stroke

- thyroid disorders

Also, many older persons think that depression is a character flaw and are worried about being teased or humiliated. They may blame themselves for their illness and are too ashamed to get help. Others worry that treatment would be too costly. Yet research has also shown that treatment is effective and, in fact, changes the brain when it works.

What are the consequences of untreated depression in older persons?

Late-life depression increases risk for medical illness and cognitive decline. Unrecognized and untreated depression has fatal consequences in terms of both suicide and nonsuicide mortality: older Caucasian males have the highest rate of suicide in the U.S. Depression is the single most significant risk factor for suicide in the elderly population. Tragically, many of those people who go on to die by suicide have reached out for help—20 percent see a doctor the day they die, 40 percent the week they die and 70 percent in the month they die. Yet depression is frequently missed. Elderly persons are more likely to seek treatment for other physical aliments than they are to seek treatment for depression.

Are symptoms of depression different in older persons than in younger persons?

Symptoms in older persons may differ somewhat from symptoms in other populations. Depression in older persons is at times characterized by:

- memory problems

- confusion

- social withdrawal

- loss of appetite

- weight loss

- vague complaints of pain

- inability to sleep

- irritability

- delusions (fixed false beliefs)

- hallucinations

Older depressed individuals often have severe feelings of sadness, but these feelings frequently are not acknowledged or openly shown; sometimes, when asked if they are depressed, the answer is "no." Some general clues that someone may be experiencing depression are:

- persistent and vague complaints

- help-seeking

- moving in a slower manner

- demanding behavior

How can clinical depression be distinguished from normal sadness and grief?

It's natural to feel grief in the face of major life changes that many elderly people experience, such as leaving a home of many years or losing a loved one. Sadness and grief are normal, temporary reactions to the inevitable losses and hardships of life. Unlike normal sadness, however, clinical depression doesn't go away by itself and lasts for months. Clinical depression needs professional treatment to reduce duration and intensity of symptoms. Any unresolved depression can affect the body. For example, depression, if left untreated, is a risk for heart disease and can suppress the immune system, raising the risk of infection.

What causes depression in older persons?

Although there is no single, definitive answer to the question of cause, many factors—psychological, biological, environmental and genetic—likely contribute to the development of depression. Scientists think that some people inherit a biological make-up that makes them more prone to depression. Imbalances in certain brain chemicals like norepinephrine, serotonin and dopamine are thought to be involved in major depression.

While some people become depressed for no easily identified reason, depression tends to run in families, and the vulnerability is often passed from parents to children. When such a genetic vulnerability exists, other factors like prolonged stress, loss or a major life change can trigger the depression. For some older people, particularly those with lifelong histories of depression, the development of a disabling illness, loss of a spouse or a friend, retirement, moving out of the family home or some other stressful event may bring about the onset of a depressive episode. It should also be noted that depression can be a side effect of some medications commonly prescribed to older persons, such as medications to treat hypertension. Finally, depression in the elderly population can be complicated and compounded by dependence on substances such as alcohol, which acts as a depressant.

Are some older persons at higher risk for depression?

Older women are at a greater risk: women in general are twice as likely as men to become seriously depressed. Biological factors, like hormonal changes, may make older women more vulnerable. The stresses of maintaining relationships or caring for an ill loved one and children also typically fall more heavily on women, which could contribute to higher rates of depression. Unmarried and widowed individuals as well as those who lack a supportive social network also have elevated rates of depression.

What Is Depression?

Major depression is a mood state that goes well beyond temporarily feeling sad or blue. It is a serious medical illness that affects one's thoughts, feelings, behavior, mood and physical health. Depression is a lifelong condition in which periods of wellness alternate with recurrences of illness. . . .

It involves some combination of the following symptoms: depressed mood (sadness), poor concentration, insomnia, fatigue, appetite disturbances, excessive guilt and thoughts of suicide.

National Alliance on Mental Illness, "
What Is Depression?," 2012. www.nami.org.

Conditions such as heart attack, stroke, hip fracture or macular degeneration and procedures such as bypass surgery are known to be associated with the development of depression. In general, depression should be assessed as a possibility if recovery from medical procedure is delayed, treatments are refused or problems with discharge are encountered.

How is depression in older persons diagnosed?

A physical exam can determine if depressive symptoms are being caused by another medical illness. Medical concerns and their treatment are common in this population. A review of the individual's medications is important: in some cases a simple medication change can reduce symptom intensity. A clinical and psychiatric interview is a key aspect of the assessment. Speaking with family members or close friends may be helpful in making a diagnosis. Blood tests and imaging studies (like a CT scan) are helpful insofar as they rule out other medical conditions that would require a different path of intervention.

Can depression in older persons be treated?

Fortunately, the treatment prognosis for depression is good. Once diagnosed, 80 percent of clinically depressed individuals can be effectively treated by medication, psychotherapy, electroconvulsive therapy (ECT) or any combination of the three. A novel treatment—transcranial magnetic stimulation (TMS)—has been approved by the FDA and may be helpful for mild depression that has not been helped by one medication trial. Medication is effective for a majority of people with depression. Four groups of antidepressant medications have been used to effectively treat depressive illness: selective serotonin re-uptake inhibitors (SSRIs); norepinephrine and serotonin re-uptake inhibitors (NSRIs); and less commonly, tricyclics and monoamine oxidase inhibitors (MAOIs). Medication adherence is especially important, but can present challenges among forgetful individuals. It is important to note that all medicines have side effects as well as benefits, and the selection of the best treatment is often made based on tolerability of the side effects. ECT (also known as shock treatment) may be very useful in the treatment of severe depression in older adults. For carefully selected people, ECT can be a lifesaving intervention. For example, an 80-year-old man who lives alone, has been depressed for months, lost 60 pounds and has delusions about his body has a kind of presentation that may improve quickly with ECT. ECT can impact memory—an important consideration in comparing it to other interventions.

Medications can be beneficial for elderly individuals in treating the symptoms of depression. Medications are frequently combined with supportive psychotherapy or cognitive behavioral therapy to improve their effectiveness. Research has shown that depressed individuals may need to try more than one medication to get an optimal response.

Psychosocial treatment plays an essential role in the care of older patients who have significant life crises, lack social support or lack coping skills to deal with their life situations.

Because large numbers of elderly people live alone, have inadequate support systems or do not have contact with a primary care physician, special efforts are needed to locate and identify these people to provide them with needed care. Natural supports like church or bridge group colleagues should be encouraged. There are services available to help older individuals, but the problem of clinical depression must be detected before treatment can begin.

Like diabetes or arthritis, depression is a chronic disease. Getting well is only the beginning of the challenge—the goal is staying well. For people experiencing their first episode of depression later in life, most experts would recommend treatment for six months to one year after acute treatment that achieves remission. For persons that have had two or three episodes during their lifetimes, treatment should extend up to two years after remission. For people with more than three recurrences of depression, treatment may be lifelong. The treatment that gets someone well is the treatment that will keep that person well.

> *"Fifteen years after Proposition 215 enshrined in the [California] state constitution a medical right to cannabis for the sick and dying, the sick and dying and just plain old have the hardest time getting it."*

Seniors Should Have Better Access to Medical Marijuana

David Downs

David Downs is a journalist and blogger. In the following viewpoint, he outlines the challenges many elderly Americans living in adult residential facilities (ARFs) face in obtaining legal medical marijuana. Downs finds that access to medical marijuana is difficult for all seniors in California, but particularly in ARFs that limit access because they depend on federal funding—which prohibits marijuana use. Some activists are stepping in to ensure that seniors with prescriptions for medical marijuana have the access they need to treat chronic conditions like cancer, glaucoma, and anxiety.

As you read, consider the following questions:

1. How many adult residential facilities (ARFs) are there in Southern California, according to Downs?

2. As reported by Downs, what is SB 420?

3. According to the author, how must ARFs receive cannabis under the law?

A tide is coming in. The Baby Boomers are retiring. When they can't live on their own, many go into what are called "adult residential facilities," or ARFs.

ARFs offer seniors their own little space. They don't have to take out the trash, or mow the lawn, or clean and wash, if they don't want to. There's someone to make sure medications are taken.

But that medication better not be cannabis.

Fifteen years after Proposition 215 enshrined in the state constitution a medical right to cannabis for the sick and dying, the sick and dying and just plain old have the hardest time getting it.

Denied Access to Legal Cannabis

Even before the 2010 crackdown, California seniors faced tough odds of access. Those odds become impossible as seniors progress along the typical path from independent living to assisted living.

Seniors in adult residential facilities—and there are 5,000 such facilities in Southern California alone—are often denied their cannabis medication, forced to medicate in back alleys, or even evicted for possessing it, according to several activists.

Which is why Pasadena activist Liz McDuffie is ecstatic to share that the California's Department of Social Services has just licensed her and her five-year-old group called the MCC Directory to teach the class "California's Medical Marijuana Program Act as It Relates to Adult Residential Care Facility Access." The class is part of mandatory continuing education curriculum for ARF operators who want to keep their state licenses.

"In order to get their renewal, there's a list of classes and they have to take 40 hours, and we're in there!" McDuffie said. It will help keep senior medical marijuana patients in their homes, she said.

State-licensed ARFs have to respect Prop 215 and SB 420, [which established California's medical marijuana program], and either accommodate a senior's medical cannabis use, or refer them to facility that does, her class teaches. It's just another step for McDuffie, who's been a medical cannabis advocate since her youth.

"Knowledge Is Power"

"Knowledge is power," she says. "I've always been an advocate of cannabis for medical use going back to 1969, having it prescribed by a German doctor in Heidelberg for migraines. It's always been medical for me. It was also always such madness—this whole thing, this whole prohibition thing on cannabis."

In 2004, McDuffie began a Master's thesis at the USC School of Public Administration—on the conflict between state and federal marijuana law. She studied the Canadian marijuana program and began opening information centers in California. They're impossible to make illegal. They don't sell marijuana. They just give away pamphlets on patients' rights under Prop 215 and SB 420, and growing classes. She began hearing a lot from ARFs.

"The reason we have this course is there's been increasing numbers of calls from these licensees saying 'How does this work? Where does the cannabis come from? Our patients want to participate in this program. What is this?'

"I've been teaching SB 420 at least twice every damn month since 2006," she says. "In order to qualify as approved vendors [for state courses] we had to be teaching the subject matter at least four years, and we have documented proof, for four years we had been teaching SB 420, so that qualified us."

"When they approved this we just about fainted," she said. "I've been out there for two years trying to bring doctors to facilities to talk to patients. This is going to be brand new to licensees. This class is now on their list of approved continuing education courses."

In addition to Prop 215 and SB 420, the course explains that patients must be enrolled in the state's medical marijuana program and have a state identification card. ARFs must receive cannabis from licensed, non-profit collectives or cooperatives, which means incorporated, by-lawed, business tax-paying dispensaries.

Fighting Ignorance

"They don't go fetch pot. They let collectives deliver it. They are entering the premises to drop off medicine and can give it directly to the operator of the facility or be allowed directly into the room."

She admits she has a lot of ignorance to peel back. At best, there currently is a "don't ask don't tell" policy in place at ARFs, she said.

Valerie Corral of the Wo/Men's Alliance for Medical Marijuana related stories of paralyzed patients forced to light up on the sidewalk, and a total lack of compassion and understanding by the corporations who run these places.

"It's bleak out there," she said.

"In general, facilities have been pretty closed to doing this," McDuffie said.

Facilities don't want to lose their state license or violate federal law, said MCC Directory member Susan O'Leary. "They think allowing safe access will somehow jeopardize their state license. They often use this as an excuse with me—saying they will lose their license to operate. Not true."

Their state license is secure, McDuffie says. "Now set before them in a very clear way is how they go about it. To have the DSS behind us on that is absolutely fantastic!"

Understanding the Law

The federal government is not interested in prosecuting individual patients, her class explains.

"We have to look to the Justice Department memo from James Cole which states clearly, the resources of the federal government are not best used in pursuing seriously ill patients trying to get this medicine following a state program. What that means is it becomes damn important to understand the true scope and parameters of the state medical marijuana program. Very few people do."

McDuffie's class is just one solution to the endemic problem of senior access. Cities that ban dispensaries severely limit access for seniors in ARFs. And seniors who progress past ARFs into more intensive forms of elder care like nursing homes, hospitals and hospices face almost zero chance they will be able to use cannabis. Federal funding flows through almost all such facilities and prohibits marijuana use.

"I think one of the greatest disappointments of the last 16 years is that we have not been able to provide sufficient access for folks at the end of life," says Stephen DeAngelo, founder of Harborside Health Center, a large dispensary in Oakland, CA. "If you take a look at the things cannabis is most effective for, it reads like a laundry list of ailments afflicting seniors: stress, depression, anxiety, pain, insomnia. This is a tremendously under-served population."

> "Older adults are more vulnerable to booze and drugs for a number of reasons: . . . [slowing] metabolism . . . co-existing medical conditions . . . isolated [living] situation . . . and because of the ways alcohol and drugs can interact with medications used to manage those problems."

Seniors Have Growing Rates of Addiction and Substance Abuse

Jennifer Matesa

Jennifer Matesa is a blogger and frequent contributor to The Fix, *a website about addiction and recovery. In the following viewpoint, she reports that a growing number of older Americans are seeking treatment for alcohol and drug addiction. The Substance Abuse and Mental Health Services Administration (SAMHSA) estimates that there is a tidal wave of addiction coming, composed of baby boomers and retirees who have developed addictions to deal with the physical and emotional stresses of aging. Matesa outlines the challenges for these older addicts, which include the physical dangers of detoxing from drugs and alcohol and the fact that Medicare does not pay for addiction treatment. Medical professionals must receive more training to recognize addiction in their older patients, and families must be vigilant to the symptoms of substance abuse, she warns.*

As you read, consider the following questions:

1. According to the Substance Abuse and Mental Health Services Administration (SAMHSA), as cited by Matesa, how many older adults will need substance abuse treatment in 2020?

2. According to population projections from the US Department of Health and Human Services' Administration on Aging and reported by Matesa, how many Americans in five will be 65 or older by 2030?

3. Why do some addiction facilities refuse to take elderly people, according to the author?

Carol Aronberg's drunkalogue is common: she grew up outside New York City in a privileged family full of drinkers; both her parents were alcoholics, and her father was a mean drunk whose verbal abuse damaged her self-esteem. Still, she went to college, got married, had kids and started a successful business. And then, eight years ago, her mother died, and Carol's drinking blossomed, and she expanded her repertoire to include drugs. Finally, after three overdoses on booze and benzodiazepines and a pharmacopeia of other pills ("the 'Cets," she calls them—Percocet, Fioricet, the combinations of painkiller or sedative with acetaminophen), she checked into rehab. Now she has 18 months clean and sober.

Here's the biggest difference between Aronberg's story and that of most alcoholics: She was 69 years old when she became an addict.

A Distributing Trend

Aronberg is part of what some analysts have described as an approaching tidal wave of addiction in America: older adults and members of the baby-boom generation now in their late 40s to their mid-60s, who develop addiction and get sober late in life.

A report issued by the Substance Abuse and Mental Health Services Administration (SAMHSA) has warned that the aging of the baby-boom generation is leading to huge increases in levels of addiction among adults over 50—a fact that, SAMHSA says, will require double the availability of treatment services by 2020. And many of these people, having come of age in the drug-friendly culture of the 1960s and 1970s, have little hesitation about popping painkillers and other pills to deal with the physical and emotional stresses of aging.

"I call it 'Pharmageddon,'" says Barbara Krantz, medical director of the Hartley Center, a nonprofit addiction treatment facility located in West Palm Beach, Fla. Hanley's Center for Older Adult Recovery was the first treatment center to pioneer programs specifically designed to help elderly and baby-boom adults recover from addiction. Krantz says Hanley's older-adult programs are always at full capacity with patients who come from the entire East, because so many older adults need treatment. "If you look at the SAMHSA data," she says, "the prediction is that five million older adults will need treatment in 2020." That's twice the number requiring treatment in 2000.

Another SAMHSA study found that drug abuse (including prescription drug abuse) among adults 50–59 jumped from 2.7 percent of that population in 2002 to 5.8 in 2010, and that among those 55 to 59, the rate roughly doubled from 1.9 to 4.1 percent.

A Tough Recovery

Aronberg traveled from her New Jersey home to spend 60 days at Hanley. She admits she was fortunate to have the resources to pay for private rehab services (at a cost of nearly $50,000). Not everyone is so lucky. Many older adults who need treatment are unable to get it due to the simple, shocking fact that Medicare does not pay for addiction treatment, says Neil Capretto, medical director of Gateway Rehabilitation in Pittsburgh, Pa. Capretto's region has the highest concentration of elderly people outside the Florida retirement communities. "I'd take Medicare, but Medicare won't take us," Capretto says. "Medicare would recognize us if we were still hospital-based." But many treatment facilities that offer "medically-monitored" detox are free-standing and independent of hospitals.

When Aronberg completed the 30-day program, she says, "I was no more ready to get out than the man in the moon," and she re-upped for another month. She had arrived not just with her alcohol addiction but also with 30 bottles of prescription drugs—after her third OD, she says, "When they swept my house, you could have sold them on the street to pay your mortgage off. The doctors never told me to stop taking anything—they kept giving me more. My daughter went to the doctor and said, 'My mom's been taking too much,' and he said, 'That might be true, but it would be harder to get her off.'"

According to Krantz, at least half of patients like Aronberg arrive at Hanley with prescription drug problems, with painkillers being the primary drug of abuse, then sedative-hypnotics (usually benzos like Xanax and Ativan). And a common misconception doctors have about addiction in older people is that you can't teach an old dog new tricks—that older folks just can't recover from addiction or deal effectively in their later years with their underlying psychological problems and life-stresses.

Factors Contributing to Addiction

It's true that older folks are experiencing more stress. A 2011 "Stress in America" survey conducted by the American Psychological Association (APA) found that older adults are trying to cope with more life-stress than ever before. The results show stress is impacting health in particular among adults 50 and older who have to care for both parents and children, and also those who have been diagnosed with obesity and/or depression.

Loneliness and isolation can contribute to depression, and elderly people are increasingly vulnerable. A recent study at the University of California, San Francisco, found that while the number of older adults who say they feel lonely hasn't changed much, the quality of health of lonely older adults has decreased: those who felt isolated said they had a harder time bathing, dressing, eating, and just getting around than those who felt connected to others. And loneliness can contribute to shame.

"Shame is the number one issue for older adults," says Carol Colleran, an international certified alcohol and drug counselor, author of a sourcebook on aging and addiction, and pioneer of Hanley's older-adult program in the 1990s. Retired from Hanley, Colleran is now helping to establish a brand-new program for those over 60 at Pine Grove Behavioral Health and Addiction Services, headquartered in Hattiesburg, Miss. "The reason for [their shame], I've realized, is that they grew up in a generation where alcoholism was not a disease—it was the town drunk, the man under the bridge. And to them, for a grandmother to be an alcoholic is a very shameful thing."

An Aging Population

Pine Grove is implementing secure, high-definition online videoconferencing as part of its intensive outpatient service to help the increasing numbers of older adults who reach out for help with addiction. According to population projections from the U.S. Department of Health and Human Services' Administration on Aging, by 2030 nearly one in five U.S. residents will

Getting Older Addicts the Help They Need

Millions of baby boomers will likely face difficulties getting diagnoses and treatment for mental health conditions and substance abuse problems unless there is a major effort to significantly boost the number of health professionals and other service providers able to supply this care as the population ages, says a new report from the Institute of Medicine. The magnitude of the problem is so great that no single approach or isolated changes in a few federal agencies or programs will address it, said the committee that wrote the report.

The report calls for a redesign of Medicare and Medicaid payment rules to guarantee coverage of counseling, care management, and other types of services crucial for treating mental health conditions and substance use problems so that clinicians are willing to provide this care. Organizations that accredit health and social service professional schools and license providers should ensure that all who see older patients—including primary care physicians, nurses, physicians' assistants, and social workers—are able to recognize signs and symptoms of geriatric mental health conditions, neglect, and substance misuse and abuse and provide at least basic care, the committee said.

Institute of Medicine, "Baby Boomers Likely to Face Inadequate Care for Mental Health, Substance Abuse," July 10, 2012. www.iom.edu.

be 65 or older. "The nation is bracing for the impact of providing health care services to these 72 million adults," the APA survey reports, "but what may be lacking is concern about the impact on caregivers." The survey shows that these caregivers report higher levels of stress, poorer health and a greater tendency than the general population to use unhealthy behaviors—including drinking and drug-use—to relieve stress. Older adults usually report lower stress levels, but people with caregiving responsibilities say they have more stress and poorer physical health than the rest of us.

"Talk about stressors," Krantz says: "Baby-boomers statistically come in with three to four times more emotional disorders. Anxiety, depression and chronic pain are the three stressors in their lives that are the most significant." Hence the painkiller problems. Baby-boomers in particular, Krantz says, are interested in using chemicals to treat their stress—they comprise the generation of "the quick fix, better living through better chemistry."

Greater Access to Drugs

Add to this, she says, the freedom with which the medical community uses drugs to treat physical and emotional problems. Addiction specialists often point out that physicians began prescribing more painkillers after the adoption in 2001 of standards by the Joint Commission mandating the assessment of pain as the fifth vital sign.

"We've gone from one extreme to the other," she says. "Before the Joint Commission implemented the fifth vital sign, the only time we prescribed [opioid] pain medications was for cancer pain."

Krantz (who herself has been recovering since 1981 from prescription drug addiction) notes that, after the advent of the fifth-vital-sign standard, pharmaceutical companies began advertising painkillers directly to consumers. And whereas patients who grew up during the Depression usually wait to see what treatments, if any, the doctor might advise, their baby-boom counterparts—armed with computer spreadsheets and Internet research—march into doctors offices asking for particular drugs.

"We started using more narcotics," she says. "But we did that in a void" of medical education about the risks of addiction. At the national prescription drug summit in April, Krantz says, NIDA Director Nora Volkow pointed out that American medical students receive roughly 7 hours of instruction about addiction. So doctors don't screen patients, particularly older patients, for risks of addiction.

"We didn't have the education to ask the appropriate questions," she says. "Our program alumni tell us that their doctors don't ask, Are you drinking? Do you have substance abuse issues in your family?'"

The Detox Problem

Older adults are more vulnerable to booze and drugs for a number of reasons: because of the way metabolism slows with age; because of coexisting medical conditions, such as high blood pressure, diabetes or psychological problems; because many older adults live in isolated situations without structure, which allows them to drink or use without anyone else noticing; and because of the ways alcohol and drugs can interact with medications used to manage those problems. All of which makes detox a trickier prospect than with a twenty- or thirty-something—especially if the patient has been using alcohol and drugs together.

"I wish they just came in on alcohol," but it's usually alcohol and benzos, alcohol and painkillers, Krantz says. Because of reduced metabolism, blood alcohol levels "are usually pretty high," Krantz says. "And then you add, for example, hypertension to that, so when you go through withdrawal, what you can expect is the exact opposite—their seizure risk is up, heart arrhythmia is up, blood pressure is up." Older patients experience greater and longer sleep disturbances, malnutrition, peripheral neuropathy, and other complications during withdrawal—problems that are best overseen by a trained staff, Krantz says.

Sharyn K., 67, is an example of how difficult it is for older people to metabolize drugs. After three surgeries left her with pain down her legs, she was prescribed dilaudid and fentanyl, two strong synthetic opioid painkillers. As Sharyn explains it, she thought she had quit drinking "the day before the first surgery" in 2009. "But I was so whacked out" on the painkillers "that I didn't know I was still drinking vodka every night," she says of her post-surgery experience. "And I was already on Valium and Xanax for anxiety."

Though she took her medications as prescribed, she continued to drink and spent two years in a fog, falling twice and injuring her head. "I didn't know where I was," she says.

Depending on the level of physical dependence, even some addiction facilities apparently won't take elderly people because of the complexities of detoxing them. Doris, a 73-year-old Atlanta grandmother and former nurse who had become addicted to methadone and fentanyl prescribed originally for arthritis and back pain, was refused admission by several local addiction facilities. She had climbed to more than 100 milligrams of methadone per day.

"Her dose was too high, and therefore a detox far too dangerous," her daughter-in-law Elizabeth says. "Anything over 35 milligrams and they won't touch her with a ten-foot pole."

Doris's family had to pay out of pocket for detox services at Emory University—and even then, Elizabeth says, Doris was so desperate for drugs that she threatened suicide, called in false prescriptions, and faked a middle-of-the-night injury at her assisted living facility to get sent to the emergency department, where, as a former nurse, she knew how to game the system for more painkillers. Doris has now successfully tapered down to 40 milligrams, Elizabeth says. The plan, she says, is to get Doris down to 10 milligrams once per day, with additional pain control provided through physical and psychological therapy.

"She is coherent now," Elizabeth says. "Her handwriting has improved dramatically, she has lost weight since she's no longer watching TV in bed all day long, and her overall mood is one of being with us instead of being obsessed about pain and pain pills." She has also stopped falling so frequently—a situation diagnosed in detox as postural hypotension resulting from excessive opioid use, Elizabeth says.

Families Urge Treatment

Krantz says 40 percent of Hanley's older adults enter treatment at the urging of family members who notice their loved one falling frequently or sustaining unexplained bruises. "Don't just chalk it off to age," she says. "You may see their hygiene declining, their memory loss increasing. They may isolate. They may have malnutrition. They may start to complain about sleep disturbances, or their other diseases may be getting worse. In these circumstances people need to start thinking about addiction."

After Sharyn fell twice, her daughter saw she needed help and got her into rehab. "I was incoherent on the phone, and if she visited me, I was always sleeping," Sharyn says. She stayed at Hanley for 113 days and went from there into an intensive outpatient program in North Carolina. Now she continues her recovery in 12-step programs. Since getting clean, she actually has less pain, and she can relate to her granddaughters, who initially were "very leery about seeing Nanny again because of the person I used to be."

Carol Aronberg made it into detox after her daughter "rescued" her when she overdosed for the third time on alcohol and pills. Her daughter found out about Hanley from a cousin in Florida and arranged for Carol's admission. She has been clean and sober since January 2011, and she and Sharyn both agree that the rehab program tailored for their generation made all the difference.

"It was important to me that I wasn't sleeping next to an 18-year-old," Sharyn says.

"You can't be in a treatment program with all different age groups. We have different needs," Aronberg says. "Our children are grown, we have grandchildren that are grown. Energy-wise, I might have fit in with the baby-boomers, but I needed to be with my own age group because of the quietness of the evenings. Fortunately I had the sense to realize that, if I'm going to be here, I'm going to get the best for me."

Among her fellow patients in the program for older adults, Aronberg noticed that, despite their relative wealth, many of them had enormous fear of growing old and not being taken care of in their age. "That loneliness was a factor" that exacerbated their addiction, she says. "There was a lot of denial. Several people did relapse. There weren't that many who had the same do-or-die attitude that I did."

Aronberg is in the process of selling her business to concentrate on her own recovery. Like many women her age, she has spent a lifetime thinking of other people, and now she's developing a new attitude. "Everybody has depended on me, and I'm done," she says. "I'm not feeling guilty about it. I'm in a phenomenal new life—I'm happy, and I have a reason to live. Instead of looking at life like, 'Why me?' I don't even think like that anymore. It's like, 'Thank you, thank you, thank you.'"

Periodical Bibliography

The following articles have been selected to supplement the diverse views presented in this chapter.

Michelle Andrews
"Few Seniors Have Long-Term Care Insurance," *Kaiser Health News*, December 14, 2010.

Stuart M. Butler
"Confronting the Problem of Long-Term Care," The Heritage Foundation, September 27, 2012.

Sanjay Gupta
"Sexual Activity and STD Rate Up Among Seniors," CNN Health, February 2, 2012.

Frederik Joelving
"Viagra-Popping Seniors Lead the Pack for STDs," Reuters, July 6, 2010.

Mark Koba
"Alzheimer's: Are We Ready for the Coming Epidemic?" CNBC.com, October 8, 2012.

Rosemary McClure
"Dealing with Depression in Seniors," *Los Angeles Times*, April 17, 2010.

Joseph Nowinski
"Over 50 and 'Almost Alcoholic,'" *The Huffington Post*, April 3, 2012.

Sandra Day O'Connor and Maria Shriver
"Curing Our Alzheimer's Epidemic," *Washington Post*, December 17, 2010.

Adrian Rogers
"Depressed Seniors Need to Be Convinced It's OK to Seek Help," *The Spokesman-Review*, December 11, 2012.

Craig Schneider
"Seniors Turn to Medicaid for Long-Term Care," *Atlanta Journal-Constitution*, November 17, 2011.

Matt Sedensky
"When Grandpa Is an Addict: Big Spike in Senior Drug Abuse," NBC News, May 18, 2011.

Kenneth Thorpe and Robert Egge
"Alzheimer's Adds to Health-Care Challenge," *El Paso Times*, November 4, 2012.

For Further Discussion

Chapter 1

1. This chapter examines several economic consequences of global aging. Which challenge do you believe is the most serious for the United States? Globally? In your own community?

2. Robert D. Hormats suggests that aging populations can drive economic growth. Eric Laursen contends that these demographic shifts can lead to an economic crisis. Which author makes a more persuasive case and why?

3. What impact does America's aging population have on Medicare? Read viewpoints written by Michael Hodin and Abdul El-Sayed to inform your answer.

Chapter 2

1. Elizabeth Rogers maintains that age discrimination in the workplace is a problem. In her viewpoint, Diana Furchtgott-Roth argues that it is not. Which do you find is the more plausible argument and why? In what fields do you think that being older would be a disadvantage?

2. After reading the viewpoints by Elaine Kurtenbach and Emily Yoffee, do you believe that local and national governments are responding adequately to challenges posed by aging populations? Why or why not? Cite examples from your own life or local community in which aging groups present a challenge that is being properly or improperly addressed?

Chapter 3

1. Chapter 3 examines the viability and effectiveness of Social Security. After reading all of the viewpoints in the

chapter, what is your opinion on Social Security? Is it a successful program? Be prepared to defend your answer.

2. What should be the future of Social Security? Laurence M. Vance contends that it should be abolished. Janice Gregory argues that it should be protected and strengthened. Which author makes the more convincing argument and why?

Chapter 4

1. Which of the medical challenges examined in this chapter do you consider to be the most serious? In your community, what medical challenges do seniors face?

2. In his viewpoint, David Downs contends that seniors should have better access to medical marijuana. Do you agree or disagree? What is the policy on medical marijuana in your state?

Organizations to Contact

The editors have compiled the following list of organizations concerned with the issues debated in this book. The descriptions are derived from materials provided by the organizations. All have publications or information available for interested readers. The list was compiled on the date of publication of the present volume; the information provided here may change. Be aware that many organizations take several weeks or longer to respond to inquiries, so allow as much time as possible.

AARP
601 E Street NW, Washington, DC 20049
(888) 687-2277
e-mail: member@aarp.org
website: www.aarp.org

Founded as the American Association of Retired Persons in 1958, AARP is a nonprofit membership organization for Americans age 50 and older thatadvocates for the rights and interests of aging men and women. Two of AARP's most important issues have been health care for seniors and protecting and strengthening Social Security and Medicare. AARP also provides discounts to members on selected products and services. It is considered one of the most powerful lobbying groups in the country, representing more than 37 million people. The AARP website features access to *AARP The Magazine, AARP The Bulletin*, podcasts and video, and a range of information on politics, travel, and culture geared toward older Americans.

Alliance for Retired Americans
815 16th Street NW, 4th Floor, Washington, DC 20006
(202) 637-5399
website: www.retiredamericans.org

The Alliance for Retired Americans is a membership organization that works to "ensure social and economic justice and full civil rights for all citizens so that they may enjoy lives of dignity, personal and family fulfillment and security." The Alliance for Retired Americans has created a grassroots movement of more than four million people to lobby for a range of issues, including the protection and strengthening of Social Security, lowering prescription drug costs, and addressing the issue of long-term health care for older Americans. The group's website features important information on retirement resources, legislative efforts, state-by-state initiatives, and breaking news. It also links to the Alliance's blog, YouTube and Flickr channels, and Twitter and Facebook pages.

American Geriatrics Society (AGS)

40 Fulton Street, 18th Floor, New York, NY   10038
(212) 308-1414 • fax: (212) 832-8646
e-mail: infoamger@americangeriatrics.org
website: www.americangeriatrics.org

The American Geriatrics Society (AGS) is a nonprofit organization of health professionals that aims to improve the "the health, independence and quality of life of all older people." To accomplish this, the group lobbies politicians, policy makers, business leaders, and the public for practical and effective programs to address needs in in-patient care, research, and education. Other endeavors of AGS are to recruit qualified and devoted health care professionals to work in the geriatric field and advocate for top-notch training and educational opportunities for geriatric health care workers. AGS publishes a quarterly newsletter, which is available on the group's website. Additional information can also be found on the website, including reports, journals, updates on programs and lobbying efforts, and an online bookstore for health care professionals.

American Medical Association (AMA)

515 N. State Street, Chicago, IL   60654
(800) 621-8335
website: www.ama-assn.org

The American Medical Association (AMA) is an association of physicians that works to "promote the art and science of medicine and the betterment of public health." One of AMA's key aims is to help doctors better help patients. AMA supports more research into the medical use of marijuana and has called the government to review the classification of cannabis as a Schedule I drag. It has also been active in improving senior medical care and supporting research into Alzheimer's and dementia. *The Journal of the American Medical Association (JAMA)* is one of several journals published by AMA; others include *American Medical News, Virtual Mentor: A Forum for Medical Ethics,* and *AMA Wire,* a weekly newsletter that features commentary and breaking medical news.

Americans for Safe Access (ASA)
1806 Vernon Street NW, Washington, DC   20009
(510) 251-1856 • fax: (202) 618-6977
e-mail: info@safeaccessnow.org
website: http://safeaccessnow.org/

Americans for Safe Access (ASA) is a membership organization devoted to ensuring safe and legal access to medical marijuana for eligible patients. ASA works to pass legislation legalizing medical marijuana through lobbying, cannabis education, and media outreach. ASA also monitors law enforcement efforts in states where marijuana is legal for medical purposes, working to defend the rights of patients and providers. ASA's recent campaigns and efforts are chronicled on the group's website, which also features a blog, forums, and information about available resources.

Gerontological Society of America (GSA)
1220 L Street NW, Suite 901, Washington, DC   20005
(202) 842-1275 • fax: (202) 842-1150
website: www.geron.org

Founded in 1945, the Gerontological Society of America (GSA) is "the oldest and largest interdisciplinary organization devoted to research, education, and practice in the field of aging." GSA's mission is to advance the study of aging and inform policy makers, educators, and the public on its findings. One of the ways it accomplishes this goal is to bring researchers, practitioners, biologists, and other health professionals together for the Annual Scientific Meeting, a conference that examines matters of interest and allows those in the gerontological field to network and exchange ideas. GSA publishes several prestigious journals, including *Journal of Gerontology: Medical Science* and *Journal of Gerontology: Biological Science*. It also offers a number of e-newsletters, including *Public Policy & Aging*, which presents key developments in aging policy, and the quarterly *Aging Means Business*, a business-oriented magazine.

Institute of Medicine (IOM)

500 Fifth Street NW, Washington, DC   20001
(202) 334-2352 • fax: (202) 334-1412
e-mail: iomwww@nas.edu
website: www.iom.edu

The Institute of Medicine (IOM) was established in 1970 as the health division of the National Academy of Sciences. IOM is an independent and nonpartisan organization that "works outside of government to provide unbiased and authoritative advice to decision makers and the public." It does this by conducting extensive research on the nation's emerging health problems and then consults with and advises policy makers and legislators on developing sound public health policy. One of its primary responsibilities is organizing forums, roundtables, conferences, seminars, and other activities that work to facilitate debate, conversation, and the exchange of information. The IOM website offers access to hundreds of in-depth reports and studies published by the organization as well as videos of lectures, speeches, and expert panels.

Mental Health America (MHA)

2000 N. Beauregard Street, 6th Floor, Alexandria, VA   22311
(703) 684-7722 • fax: (703) 684-5968
e-mail: infoctr@mentalhealthamerica.net
website: www.nmha.org

Mental Health America (MHA), formerly known as the National Mental Health Association, is a nonprofit advocacy organization dedicated to helping people live mentally healthier lives. MHA works to educate and advocate for effective and fair mental health programs and policies, including suicide outreach and prevention; to support individuals and families living with mental health and substance use problems; and to end discrimination against people with mental and addictive disorders. The MHA website features the latest news, fact sheets on key issues, educational materials, position briefs, a blog, and updates on recent events. MHA also publishes *The Bell*, which offers information on the organization's recent efforts.

National Committee to Preserve Social Security and Medicare (NCPSSM)
10 G Street NE, Suite 600, Washington, DC   20002
(202) 216-0420 • fax: (202) 216-0446
e-mail: websmaster@ncpssm.org
website: www.ncpssm.org

The National Committee to Preserve Social Security and Medicare (NCPSSM) is a membership organization founded to "protect, preserve, promote, and ensure the financial security, health, and the well-being of current and future generations of maturing Americans." The NCPSSM advocates for policies that support Social Security and Medicare, not privatize or abolish it. It also works to better educate voters on the importance of Social Security and Medicare, analyze reform plans to both programs, and lobby for sensible and beneficial reforms. The NCPSSM website offers information on how to get involved in upcoming campaigns, features a blog that reports and comments on breaking news, and provides resources for those interested in the group's initiatives.

National Council on Aging (NCOA)
1901 L Street NW, 4th Floor, Washington, DC   20036
(202) 479-1200
website: www.ncoa.org

The National Council on Aging (NCOA) is a nonprofit advocacy organization that aims to provide a voice for older Americans and community organizations involved in providing services to them. NCOA surveys the needs of America's aging population and brings businesses, nonprofit organizations, and national, state, and local governments together to meet those needs and improve the quality of their lives. Some specific goals include preserving and strengthening Social Security and Medicare; passing legislation to improve options for long-term medical care for seniors; educating older Americans on how to prevent falls, treat diabetes, and prevent suicide; and providing resources to caregivers and families. The NCOA website features the latest news relevant to older Americans, press releases, a calendar of upcoming events, and a link to the NCOA YouTube channel, which offers a range of helpful and informative videos.

Substance Abuse and Mental Health Services Administration (SAMHSA)

PO Box 2345, Rockville, MD   20847
(877) 726-4727 • fax: (240) 221-4292
e-mail: SAMHSAInfo@samhsa.hhs.gov
website: www.samhsa.gov

The Substance Abuse and Mental Health Services Administration (SAMHSA) is an agency of the Department of Health and Human Services that was created to focus attention, programs, and funding on improving the lives of people with or at risk for mental and substance abuse disorders. SAMHSA publishes statistics on the epidemic of prescription drug abuse and other substances on its website. SAMHSA publications can be found at the National Clearinghouse for Alcohol and Drug Information. Many of these works are available via webcast or digital download. The website links to the SAMHSA Substance Abuse Treatment Locator, which helps users find a treatment center near them.

US Department of Health and Human Services (HHS)

200 Independence Ave. SW, Washington, DC   20201
(877) 696-6775
website: www.hhs.gov

The Department of Health and Human Services (HHS) is the US government agency in charge of protecting the health of and providing essential health services to all Americans. HHS works closely with state and local governments to develop programs and implement policies. The HHS website features information for aging Americans, including fact sheets on vaccinations like the seasonal flu shot, briefings and video reports on the Affordable Care Act (ACA) and Medicare reform, promotion of senior nutrition information and resources on alcohol and prescription drug abuse, and reporting on the disturbing trend of elder abuse and efforts to address the problem.

Bibliography of Books

Stuart A. Altman and David Shactman — *Power, Politics, and Universal Health Care: The Inside Story of a Century-Long Battle.* Amherst, NY: Prometheus Books, 2011.

Greg Campbell — *Pot, Inc.: Inside Medical Marijuana, America's Most Outlaw Industry.* New York: Sterling, 2012.

Margaret Cruikshank — *Learning to Be Old: Gender, Culture, and Aging.* 3rd ed. Lanham, MD: Rowman & Littlefield, 2013.

Scott Davidson — *Going Grey: The Mediation of Politics in an Ageing Society.* Burlington, VT: Ashgate, 2012.

Ted C. Fishman — *Shock of Gray: The Aging of the World's Population and How It Pits Young Against Old, Child Against Parent, Worker Against Boss, Company Against Rival, and Nation Against Nation.* New York: Scribner, 2010.

John Geluardi — *Cannabiz: The Explosive Rise of the Medical Marijuana Industry.* Sausalito, CA: Polipoint Press, 2010.

Michael Gurian — *The Wonder of Aging: A New Approach to Embracing Life.* New York: Atria Books, 2013.

Robert B. Hudson, ed. — *The New Politics of Old Age Policy.* 2nd ed. Baltimore: Johns Hopkins University Press, 2010.

Patricia Kolb — *Understanding Aging and Diversity: Theories and Concepts*. London: Routledge, 2013.

Jonathan V. Last — *What to Expect When No One Is Expecting: America's Coming Demographic Disaster*. New York: Encounter Books, 2013.

Martin A. Lee — *Smoke Signals: A Social History of Marijuana—Medical, Recreational & Scientific*. New York: Scribner, 2012.

Ronald Lee and Andrew Mason — *Population Aging and Generational Economy: A Global Perspective*. Cheltenham, UK: Edward Elger, 2011.

Meika Loe — *Aging Our Way: Lessons for Living from 85 and Beyond*. New York: Oxford University Press, 2011.

Frederick R. Lynch — *One Nation Under AARP: The Fight over Medicare, Social Security, and America's Future*. Berkeley: University of California Press, 2011.

Susan A. McDaniel and Zachary Zimmer, eds. — *Global Ageing in the Twenty-First Century: Challenges, Opportunities, and Implications*. Burlington, VT: Ashgate, 2013.

Carol Orsborn — *Fierce with Age: Chasing God and Squirrels in Brooklyn*. New York: Turner, 2013.

Fred Pearse — *The Coming Population Crash and Our Planet's Surprising Future*. Boston: Beacon Press, 2010.

Amanda Phelan	*International Perspectives on Elder Abuse.* New York: Routledge, 2013.
Chris Phillipson	*Ageing.* Cambridge, UK: Polity, 2013.
Jason L. Powell, ed.	*Understanding Aging: A Short Tour.* Hauppauge, NY: Nova Science, 2013.
Lynn Segal	*Out of Time: The Pleasures and Perils of Aging.* Brooklyn: Verso, 2013.
Janet Yagoda Shagam	*An Unintended Journey: A Caregiver's Guide to Dementia.* Amherst, NY: Prometheus Books, 2013.
Janet M. Wilmoth and Kenneth F. Ferraro, eds.	*Gerontology: Perspectives and Issues.* 4th ed. New York: Springer, 2013.
Kristine Yaffe, ed.	*Chronic Medical Disease and Cognitive Aging: Toward a Healthy Body and Brain.* New York: Oxford University Press, 2013.
Alex Zhavoronkov	*The Ageless Generation: How Advances in Biomedicine Will Transform the Global Economy.* New York: Palgrave Macmillan, 2013.

Index

N